Critical

Thinking

The Best Beginner's Guide To Improve Your Skills Of Problem Solving Logically. Increase Your Independent Thinking Skills And Decision Making Abilities

ROY J. DERRY

The trademarks that are used are without any consent, and the publication of the trademark is without permission or backing by the trademark owner. All trademarks and brands within this book are for clarifying purposes only and are the owned by the owners themselves, not affiliated with this document

Table Of Contents

Introduction

Critical thinking is a process that is very involved in gaining understanding, gaining knowledge, and solving problems. The method of critical thinking requires an open mind when gathering and analyzing data to consider many possible solutions to the questions raised. The process requires a thorough evaluation of each likely answer for the probability of accuracy. This process is accomplished by picking the answer with the highest probability of precision.

For example, thinking is something we all do. There are likely variations in our thought from our prejudices and distorted views. The prejudices or skewed perceptions may be based on assumptions that we have made and facts that we have accepted as true. Questioning our assumptions and the information given to us will help us carry out assessments that may foster our ability to gain value from our thinking. Because our thought outcomes determine how effective we are to be, it is very necessary to improve our ability to think (i.e., Our ability to think critically).

In many respects, thinking is a higher-order cognitive ability, which consists primarily of analyzing claims and making judgments that can lead to convictions being formed. Others feel it is to use reasoning skills to identify and analyze arguments. All views require the analysis of claims.

To assess whether the knowledge meets the Universal Intellectual Requirements, statements must be tested. The Universal Intellectual Standard measure knowledge value. This definition encourages critical thinking. Assessment of Uniform Intellectual Standards:

The specificity of information-seeks elaboration

> The reliability of information-seeks confirmation

> The quality of information-seeks details

> The importance of information-seeks a link

> The breadth of information-seeks concern of nuances

> The air of information-seeks other points of view

> The rationality of information-seeks continuity

> Importance of information-seeks

In an attempt to clarify the skills involved in critical thinking, several other theories have arisen. One concept includes interpretation (categorization, decoding of meaning, and clarification of meaning); analysis (examination of ideas, identification of arguments, and analysis of arguments); evaluation (evaluation of claims and evaluation of arguments); inference (examination of evidence, conjecture of alternatives, and drawing of conclusions); explanation (setting of results, justifying procedures, and presenting arguments); While the skills involved in critical thinking may be explained by these concepts, the critical thinking process can be explained more clearly.

What Is Critical Thinking?

Can you end up with specific outcomes if you solve problems? To come to your conclusions, do you use logic, analysis, and evaluation? Have you always arrived at a realistic and rational approach to your problems? If you do, you're thinking critically. Another concept is being able to effectively use your cognitive abilities to achieve a specific goal. In other words, critical thinking does not waste much time, but rather focuses on the necessary aspects of a problem to quickly and efficiently arrive at an actual solution.

The ability to think clearly and rationally about what to do or believe is critical thinking. It includes the ability to think reflectively and independently. The following can be achieved by someone with skills:

- ➤ Considering the logical connections among concepts
- ➤ Recognizing, building and testing claims
- ➤ Finding discrepancies or specific flaws of thinking
- ➤ Regularly solving problems

- ➢ Defining the significance or usefulness of ideas
- ➢ Focusing on defending one's own beliefs and values

Critical thinking is not about gathering information. In critical thinking, a person with a good memory who knows a lot of facts is not necessarily good. A serious thinker can deduce consequences from what he knows, and he knows how to use the information to solve problems and search for relevant information sources to inform himself.

Thinking should not be confused with complaining or judging others. Although it is possible to use critical thinking skills to expose errors and bad reasoning, critical thinking can also play an important role in cooperative reasoning and constructive tasks. Thinking will help us gain knowledge, strengthen our ideas, and support claims. To strengthen job practices and improve social institutions, they can use critical thinking.

Some people believe that critical thinking hinders creativity because it requires logic and rationality rules to be followed, but creativity may require rules that break. This is confusion. Critical thinking is consistent with "out-of-the-box" thinking, challenging consensus, and pursuing less popular approaches. If anything, critical thinking is an essential part of innovation because to analyze and develop our creative ideas, and we need critical thinking.

Critical thinking is the scientifically focused method of conceptualizing, applying, interpreting, synthesizing, and assessing the information collected from, or created by, interpretation, practice, thought, logic, or interaction as a guide to belief and action. It is based on its exemplary nature on common cognitive principles that surpass distinctions of subject matter: transparency, reliability, accuracy, integrity, validity, solid proof, good reasons, scope, width, and equity.

It involves examining those structures are thought elements implied in all reasoning: purpose, problem, or question-at-issue; assumptions; concepts; empirical grounding; reasoning leading to conclusions; implications and consequences; objections from alternative points of view; and frame of reference. Critical thinking — in response to complex themes, problems, and purposes — is embedded in a family of interwoven modes of thinking, including scientific thinking, analytical thinking, historical thinking, anthropological thinking, economic thinking, ethical thinking, and theoretical thinking.

It can be view as having two components: 1) a collection of skills producing and processing information and conviction, and 2) the practice of using those skills to direct actions, based on cognitive dedication. It is, therefore, to be compared with 1) the pure collection and storage of information alone, because it implies a particular way in which information is obtained and treated; 2) the mere ownership of a set of skills, because it requires the constant use of them; and 3) the mere use of those skills ("as an exercise") without the recognition of their performance.

Thinking varies depending on the underlying motivation. Built-in selfish motives, it is often reflected in the ability to manipulate information in the name of the vested interest of one's own, or of one's classes. It is typically intellectually flawed as such, though it might be pragmatically successful. It is usually of a higher order scientifically if rooted in faithfulness and moral honesty, although susceptible to the allegation of "idealism" by those accustomed to its greedy application.

In any adult, critical thinking of any kind is not universal; each is subject to outbreaks of undisciplined or irrational thinking. Hence, its quality is typically a matter of degree and depends, among other things, on the quality and depth of experience in a given field of thinking or on a particular class of questions. No one is a critical thinker through-and-through, but only to such an extent, with such-and-such observations and blind spots, prone to such-and-such self-delusion habits. For this cause, it is a life-long goal to improve critical thinking skills and dispositions.

Another Brief Conceptualization of Critical Thinking

Critical thinking is self-guided, self-disciplined thinking that tries to reason in a fair-minded way at the highest quality level. Those who regularly think critically try to live in a moral, compassionate, empathetic way. If left unchecked, we are keenly aware of the inherently flawed nature of human thought. They strive to diminish the power of their tendencies that are egocentric and sociocentric. We use the analytical methods provided by critical thinking–theories and values that help them to assess, examine, and improve learning.

We are working diligently to cultivate the academic values of intellectual integrity, intellectual modesty, intellectual morality, intellectual conscience, intellectual sense of justice, and faith in reason. We know that no matter how skilled we are as analysts, they can always improve their ability to reason, and sometimes they will be vulnerable to logical errors, human irrationality, assumptions, stereotypes, misconceptions, uncritically accepted social norms, and abuses, self-interest, and vested interest.

They are striving to improve the environment and lead to a more moral, civilized society in whatever way they can.   At the same time, we understand the often underlying challenges of doing so.   They avoid thinking about complicated issues in a simplistic manner and strive to take proper account of the rights and needs of relevant others.   I understand the challenges of evolving as individuals and are committed to life-long self-improvement training.

How to Learn the Basics of Psychology

Psychology is one of the world's most popular subjects in college and university campuses, but that doesn't mean you have to pursue a psychology degree to know more about the human mind and behavior. There are many interesting ways to learn more about the human mind and actions now, such as completing a college course, signing up for a free online class, or using online resources to educate yourself.

For many, and for a good reason, psychology is a subject of interest. Through learning more about the fundamentals of the human mind and actions, people will gain a better understanding of themselves and others. Psychologists also play a vital role in the health care system by assisting people with mental health problems, administering psychotherapy, researching different treatment options, and advising patients on how to effectively manage their symptoms.

Introduction to Psychology

It's always a good idea to start with the basics when learning something new. Learn more about what the history of psychology is.

Spend some time learning more about what psychology is as well as the early history of the subject as you begin your investigation into this topic. The major topic that also covers nearly every introductory psychology class at the outset is a description of the many different branches of psychology.

Psychological research methodology How do scientists study human behavior? To think more about how and why people behave as they do, every psychology student must have a basic understanding of the research methods used by psychologists.

Even if you are not intending to become a research psychologist, reading more about how psychologists view the study of human behavior will give you a greater appreciation of the results that you will discover during your studies.

The scientific method and the psychology experiment cycle were important aspects of developing an understanding of how psychologists are studying the brain and actions.

Developmental Psychology

Throughout human history, not so long ago, most people believed that infants were just small adult copies. Researchers began to realize that childhood is a unique and important part of life only fairly recent. Developmental psychology is one of psychology's main subfields that focuses on all aspects of development and transition over the entire lifespan.

Developmental psychology research may seem easy; after all, we've all been through it. When you start exploring the subject, you will learn quickly that there is more to the creation thesis than you might have thought.

While reading about some of the main concepts of child development, recognizing some of the important issues and issues that affect developmental psychologists is also necessary. It involves the topic of age-old nature versus nurture, which reflects on the comparative roles of genetics and the environment.

Behavioral Psychology

Behavioral psychology is, during the 20th century, a significant school of thought that continues to be prominent today, also known as behaviorism. Many behavioral principles, including therapy, education, and animal training, are still widely used today.

Behaviorism may not be as dominant as it once was, but if you want to learn more about psychology, you still need to understand the basic principles of behavior.

Start by learning more about important concepts such as modern conditioning and conditioning for operators. Read more about the different types of reward and discipline in addition to knowing about these social coping strategies.

Important Psychology Theories and Theorists Some of the most prominent psychology theorists, including Freud, Erikson, and Piaget, have suggested theories to describe different aspects of creation, behavior, and other subjects. Although some hypotheses are no longer popular, researching the impact these ideas had on psychology is still important.

Some of the key concepts you must study include:

> Freud's Theory of Psychosexual Behavior
> Piaget's Theory of Psychological Development
> Maslow's Hierarchy of Needs
> Kohlberg's Theory of Social Development
> Big 5 Theory of Personality

Personality Psychology

Psychology of personality is another major psychological topic of interest. As you learn more about psychology, you will find that some of the best-known theories of psychologists are focused on understanding how personality evolves.

Our personality is what makes us who we are. What factors affect the shape of our personalities? Is there a set temperament, or can it change?

It is important to concentrate on some of the key topics, such as characteristics and various personality disorders, to research personality.

Social Psychology

Why do people in large groups sometimes act differently? Social psychologists are trying to understand social behavior, including how we interact with others and how others influence our behavior.

Social psychology is a fascinating field that explores a wide range of social practices, including subjects such as the influence of the bystander, beliefs, and interpretation of the individual.

Basic Psychology Facts You Need to Know

For some people, a desire to pursue a career in the field stimulates an interest in psychology. Others may want to know more out of curiosity or because they're talking about visiting a health concern therapist. Whatever the cause, building a better understanding of issues such as sentiment, inspiration, intellect, affection, interaction, and research methods in many different areas of life will serve you well.

At first, psychology may seem like a huge and overwhelming field, but it may be easier to get started by learning a few basic facts. The following are just a few important things about this fascinating topic that you need to learn. Once you have a strong understanding of the basics, you'll be better prepared to explore various ways that psychology can help improve your daily life, health, and well-being.

There has not always been science as it has now. It is considered a relatively young discipline, although it has a short past a long history, as one eminent psychologist has explained.

While in the grand scheme of things, psychology may be a young subject, it has grown to play a tremendous role in today's world. Psychologists are working in hospitals, mental health clinics, schools, colleges, and institutions, government agencies, private enterprises, and private practice, undertaking a broad range of tasks and positions ranging from mental illness care to public health policy impact.

Psychology Relies on Scientific Methods

One of the most common myths of psychology is that it's just "common sense." The trouble with this is that psychological research has helped show that many of the things we believe are common sense are not valid at all. After all, if common sense were as common as people say it is, then people wouldn't engage in behaviors they know are bad for them like eating junk food or smoking.

Psychology depends on scientific methods to analyze problems and reach conclusions, unlike common sense. Scientists were able to discover relationships between different variables by using empirical methods. Psychologists use a range of techniques, including naturalistic analysis, tests, case studies, and questionnaires, to research the human mind and behavior.

Psychologists Approach Questions From Different Perspectives

It is possible to look at subjects and problems of psychology in various ways. Let's take as an example the issue of violence.

Many psychologists may investigate how genetic causes lead to aggression, while others may analyze how factors such as family history, relationships, social pressure, and contextual variables affect violence.

Some of the main psychological perspectives include the following:
- ➤ Biological Perspective
- ➤ Cognitive Perspective
- ➤ Evolutionary Perspective
- ➤ Humanistic Perspective

Each perspective adds to a new dimension of understanding of the subject.

For example, consider that psychologists are trying to understand the multiple factors that contribute to harassment. Some scientists may look at how genes and the brain relate to this type of behavior from a biological perspective. Another counselor can take a psychological approach to look at the various ways the climate promotes harassment behaviors. Other researchers can take a social perspective and examine the potential impact of group pressure on bullying behaviors.

No one viewpoint is "right." It adds to how we interpret an issue and helps scientists to examine the various factors that lead to certain activities and seek multi-faceted approaches to combat problem actions and encourage better outcomes and healthy habits.

Psychiatry Is All Around You

Psychology is not just an academic subject that only resides in schools, research laboratories, and offices of mental health. Through everyday situations you can see the ideals of psychology all around you.

If you have a question, there is likely a psychiatrist who can assist there are many different types of psychologists; each focused on solving various types of word problems. For example, if your child has problems at school, you may be looking for advice from a school psychologist who specializes in helping children cope with educational, personal, psychological, and other issues. If you are concerned about an elderly parent or grandparent, you may want to seek advice from a developmental psychologist who is specially trained and knowledgeable about the aging process.

It helps to understand some of the different training and licensing requirements for different specialty areas to determine which professional is right for your needs. If you're looking to find a psychotherapist, reading more about which practitioners can provide therapy services may also be useful.

If you're talking about psychology majoring, then you should be happy to find out that there are a lot of career paths to choose from. Different career opportunities depend largely on your educational level and work experience, so it is important to research your chosen specialization area's required training and licensing requirements.

Psychologists Focus on Making Human Lives Better

The main goals of psychology are identified, illustrating, understanding, and changing human behavior. By contributing to our basic understanding of how people think, feel, and behave, some psychologists do this. In practical contexts, other therapists seek to address real-world problems that affect daily life.

And finally, many psychologists are dedicating their lives to helping people with psychological problems. Throughout hospitals, mental health centers, private practices, and other places, you can meet these professionals working to treat psychological disorders and provide psychotherapy for people from all walks of life.

Cognitive Psychology

Why are they going to forget? Why are we remembering? You can explain all this and more by learning more about a topic called cognitive psychology. Cognitive Psychology is the study of how we as humans stores information, how we learn, how we perceive, and how we input sensory. This branch of psychology allows long-term and short-term memory to be measured.

Did you know that information needs to stay long enough in the short-term memory to store something in a person's long-term memory? That's why it's hard to remember when you can't focus on facts. If the attention of a person is broken, interfered with by a distraction, the piece of information in the short-term memory may be lost forever. But, if the person can retain long enough exposure to the data, then the information will be transferred to the long-term safekeeping memory. The long-term memory has a much larger capacity, and more data is stored. Certain Cognitive Psychology subtopics include intelligence assessment and human development research.

Measurements of intelligence are more often called assessments of knowledge. These methods are very useful in determining the cognitive ability of a person. The IQ test can help teachers and parents determine what level of performance a student can predict.

Intelligence theories in cognitive psychology state that people are born with a certain range of intelligence possibilities. It is assumed that this range is largely influenced by genetic factors. The level at which the maturity of an adult is established then largely depends on environmental factors such as how the infant is born, the consumption of nutrition / physical and brain development, and the degree to which the child is intellectually challenged by the environment in which he or she resides. Cognitive psychology allows such factors to be determined.

What is the Neuroscience of Cognitive?
Cognitive psychology involves studying internal mental processes— all things that take place within your brain, including perception, thinking, memory, attention, language, problem-solving, and learning. Although it is a relatively young psychology branch, it has rapidly grown into one of the most popular subfields.

Cognitive psychology is a scientific branch and is generally used within psychology as a central field. It is one of the psychology's major branches that has provided enormous aspirant job opportunities. This usually focuses on issues related to learning, retrieval of information, mechanisms of thought, expression, language, and other aspects such as problem-solving and decision making. In this branch of psychology, individuals who make their careers are called cognitive psychologists. Our main responsibility is to investigate internal mental mechanisms, such as the role of thought, speech, interpretation, and memory. Their work is to examine how people work out on different issues by using knowledge and making decisions. Their research primarily explores how data is stored and understood by individuals.

Today it is one of the prime psychology fields and core disciplines that has attracted the attention of many U.S. youths. Also, in the last few years, after understanding the limitations of behaviorism, behavioral psychologists have gained ample support from scientists. Psychologists ' job opportunities are steadily rising and will always be plentiful as long as personal, social, and economic instability in human society prevails.

There are many practical applications for this behavioral work, such as helping to deal with memory problems, improving consistency in decision-making, discovering ways to help people heal from brain injury, managing learning disabilities, and structuring academic curricula to improve performance.

Understanding more about how people think and process information not only helps scientists get a deeper understanding of how the human brain works, but it also encourages therapists to develop new ways to help people deal with psychological problems. By recognizing, for example, that attention is both a selective and limited resource, psychologists can come up with solutions that make it easier for people with careful difficulties to improve their focus and concentration.

Cognitive psychology findings have also enhanced our understanding of how memories are formed, stored, and remembered by people. By learning more about how these processes work, psychologists can develop new ways to help people improve their memories and fight potential problems with memory.

For instance, psychologists have found that while your short-term memory is quite short and limited (which lasts only 20 to 30 seconds and can hold between five and nine items), rehearsal strategies can improve the chances of transferring information to long-term memory, which is much more stable and durable.

While many behavioral psychologists are trained in research and hired by schools and government agencies, others are having a medical approach or working directly with people who are undergoing problems related to various mental processes. We may be working in hospitals, centers for mental health, or in private practice.

Psychologists working in this area often focus on a specific area of interest, such as memory, while others may choose to work directly on specific cognition-related health concerns such as degenerative brain disorders or brain injuries.

Reasons to Consult a Cognitive Psychologist

> To treat a psychological illness with cognitive therapy methods
> To explore treatment options for brain trauma

- If you are experiencing perceptual or sensory issues
- As part of therapy for a speech or language disorder
- If you are experiencing Alzheimer's disease, dementia, or memory loss
- To explore different interventions for learning disabilities

The work of cognitive psychologists is essential for helping people who have experienced issues with mental processes. While we tend to take skills such as attention and problem solving as a matter of course, perhaps because they are so woven into the fabric of our daily existence, cognitive disruptions can create havoc in multiple areas of the life of an individual. Attention issues can make focusing on work or school difficult. Only relatively minor issues with memory can make it a struggle to tackle daily life's demands.

Remember, for instance, that your health and wellbeing may be influenced by negative thinking. From time to time, we all have these negative thoughts, but some people may be overcome by depressive habits of thinking that make it difficult to work in everyday life.

Impact of Cognitive Science on Mental Health Interventions The field of cognitive psychology has also had an impact on mental health interventions as well as contributing to the understanding of how the human mind functions. Before the 1970s, most approaches to mental health were more based on psychoanalytic, psychological, and humanistic approaches.

During this time, the so-called "cognitive revolution" put a greater focus on understanding how people process information and how patterns of thought can lead to psychological distress. New treatment strategies have been developed to help treat depression, anxiety, phobias, and other psychological disorders due to research in this area by behavioral psychologists.

Cognitive-behavioral therapy and objective cognitive behavioral therapy are two approaches that concentrate on the unconscious cognitions that lead to psychological distress by patients and counselors.

If you experience symptoms of a psychological disorder that would benefit from the use of cognitive approaches, you may see a psychologist having specific training in these methods of cognitive therapy. These professionals often have titles other than cognitive psychologists, such as a psychiatrist, clinical psychologist, or psychologist counseling, but many of the strategies they use are rooted in the cognitive tradition. If you are unsure of the discipline or approach of a practitioner, ask him or her.

What to do if you have been recently diagnosed with a cognitive issue

It can be terrifying and sometimes overwhelming to be diagnosed with a neurological or mental health problem, but it is important to remember that you are not alone.

You can build an effective treatment strategy by consulting with your doctor to help resolve brain health and cognitive issues. Your treatment may involve consulting with a cognitive psychologist who has a background in the particular area of concern you face, or you may be referred to another mental health professional who has training and experience with your particular disease.

You can find it helpful to know as much as you can about your initial diagnosis and consider creating a list of questions you have with your psychiatrist, clinical therapist, and mental health professional before your next appointment. This can help you feel more prepared and ready in your recovery for the next phase.

Overview

As you can see, the world of cognitive psychology is broad and diverse, but it influences so many areas of everyday life.

Studies on cognitive psychology may sometimes appear abstract or distant from the problems you face in everyday life, but outcomes from such scientific research play a role in how clinicians view mental illness recovery, traumatic brain injury, and degenerative brain disorders. Thanks to cognitive psychologists ' research, they can better identify ways to measure individual intellectual abilities, develop new approaches to combat memory issues, and decipher human brain functions — all of which potentially have a powerful impact on how we treat cognitive disorders.

The field of cognitive psychology is a fast-growing area that aims to contribute to our awareness of the many effects mental processes have on our health and everyday life. Through understanding that cognitive processes change throughout child development to seeing how the mind converts sensory inputs into experiences, cognitive psychology has helped us achieve a deeper and richer understanding of the many psychological events that lead to our daily existence and general well-being.

Fascinating Facts About Human Psychology

The human brain is an interesting and powerful organ, but it is a process that we are still studying to understand why it does what it does. Both the awareness and the unconscious mind have a significant impact on our actions, but most of us only have a minimal understanding of how they function.

Unless it's ourselves, we blame the actions of an individual on their temperament.

Has anyone ever cut you off at a roundabout or intersection, and made you mad, just for you to go in just 10 minutes later to do the same thing to someone else? Even though you've been angry with the person who cut you off, you're likely to justify your actions to yourself because you're "in a hurry, and that's just that once." We tend to attribute our bad behavior to external forces and the bad behavior of other people to their internal attributes.

We don't predict our reaction to future events very well.

We always think we're going to respond to a future event in a certain manner, only for the event to take place, and we're going to find that's handled very differently than we've expected. We place hope in a single occurrence's ability to change everything, but we often find that changing how we feel at all doesn't do much.

Generally, our strongest memories are right.

We feel like memories of "burn" traumatic events in our minds to stay there forever (known as "Flashbulb Memories"). Studies have shown that the more inaccurate the memory is, the stronger the emotional state you were during that event.

Only for 10 minutes, can we maintain a high concentration level.

Do you think you can focus more than 10 minutes on a task? Studies show otherwise. For average, after 10 minutes, a person's concentration period ends, then the mind starts wandering

Our brains wander for about 30% of the day.

We spend about 30% of our daydreaming on average (although some people do more). The downside of this is that experts point out that people who are more likely to daydream are better at solving challenges and are more imaginative.

Multitask is not possible for humans!

You might hear people pretending to be professional multitaskers, and in some job requirements, you likely even saw that, but humans cannot multitask. Yes, while you're busy, you can listen to music, but your mind can only perform one task at a time. Which means either you're going to do research and forget the music or listen to the music and neglect the work. There are simply two things people can't think of at once.

Most of the decisions you make are made subconsciously.

Should you think of all the decisions you make, consider all the alternatives, and quantify every outcome's impact? You may think you're, but you're right. Most of your decisions are made in your subconscious because otherwise, information would overwhelm your conscious mind and you are likely to be mentally frozen. That's because the mind absorbs more than 11 million bits of information per second, and there's not enough "brain power" to go through it all.

We can only store between 5 and 9 bits of information at once.

Only once in their short-term memory, the average human can hold an average of 7 bits of information.

Many pieces of relevant data may consist of each of the 7 bits of information. Recalling a phone number is the best example–it can be between 9 and 14 digits long anywhere, and we divide it into sections like country code, area code, and a series of numbers which we split (usually in 3-4 digit groups).

We think it's easier to influence other people than us.

We can see more plainly the influence of marketing on others than its effects on ourselves. This is defined as the Influence of the Third Person. They can see how an ad impacts our colleagues but ignores its impact on ourselves, and it gets worse when it's an ad we're not interested in for something. You still haven't noticed this, but all the commercials you see every day have an unconscious influence on your mood, your expectations, and even your mindset.

When you're asleep, the brain doesn't stop working.

As you sleep, the brain is just as active as when you're awake. Scientists have found that when you rest, the only time the brain filters away toxins and waste. It is also assumed that your mind can work out all the information from the day before and create new memories during the sleep cycles.

You get more creative when you're tired.

When you want to do something artistic, such as composing a short story or designing an outfit, after a long and stressful day, you'd be better off doing it. This is because researchers have found that when their minds do not work as well, people become more innovative. This is one of the main reasons why people often get great ideas after a hard day's work while taking a shower.

The brain feels the physical pain of rejection.

At some point in their lives, everyone feels the great pain of rejection, but did you know that rejection triggers not only emotional pain but also actual physical harm? Even if you can't feel the physical pain, scientists have found that after being rejected and feeling physical pain, the impulses and cascading events that occur in the brain are almost similar. What's more, in both cases, the same natural chemical is also released.

Relationships are as important as diet and exercise for your health.

Studies at the Chapel Hill University of North Carolina recently found that the quality and size of a person's social ties directly affect certain types of health behaviors, such as diabetes and abdominal obesity, at various points in their lives. Similarly, studies also show that being considerably lonely can reduce your life expectancy significantly.

It is more likely that smart people think they are not smart.

A phenomenon known as the Dunning Kruger Effect shows that not only do clever people tend to underestimate themselves much more than the average person, but that ignorant people prefer to overestimate themselves.

Your decisions are made more logical by speaking in a foreign language.

A series of experiments led by University of Chicago's Boaz Keysar showed that speaking in a foreign language reduced the intrusion of deceptive and deep-seated stereotypes believed to distort the interpretation of benefits and disadvantages.

Psychological Studies That Will Change The Way You Think About Yourself

Why are we doing the things we're doing? The fact is that, despite our best attempts to "learn ourselves," we still know very little about our minds, and even less about how others feel. As Charles Dickens once put it, "A marvelous reality to dwell on, that every human being is constituted to be that dark secret and mystery to each other." Psychologists have long sought insights into how we perceive the world and what motivates our behavior, and they have made tremendous strides to raise the curtain of mystery. Some of the most popular psychological experiments of the past century, apart from offering fodder to inspire cocktail party discussions, expose fundamental and often shocking facts about human nature. Here are ten classic psychological studies that can improve your self-understanding.
We all have the power to do good.

The 1971 Stanford prison research, arguably the most famous experiment in psychology, history put a spotlight on how social situations could affect human behavior. The researchers, led by psychologist Philip Zimbardo, established a mock prison in the basement of the psychic building at Stanford and selected 24 undergraduates (who had no criminal record and were considered psychologically healthy) to act as prisoners and guards. Researchers then used hidden cameras to observe the prisoners (who had to stay 24 hours a day in the cells) and guards (who shared eight-hour shifts).

The trial, planned to last for two weeks, had to be cut short after just six days due to the abusive behavior of the guards— in some situations, they also administered psychological torture— and the prisoners ' extreme emotional stress and anxiety.

"The guards intensified their aggression against the prisoners, stripping them naked, placing bags over their heads, and finally having them engage in increasingly humiliating sexual activity," Zimbardo told American Scientist.

We don't notice what's right in front of us.

Do you think you know what's happening around you? You may not be as aware as you think. Harvard and Kent State University researchers approached tourists on a college campus in 1998 to assess how much people notice of their immediate surroundings. An actress came to a pedestrian in the study and asked for directions. Two people carrying a large wooden door passed between the actor and the pedestrian while the pedestrian was providing the instructions, blocking their sight of each other for several seconds.
During that time, another actor, one of a different height and structure, and with a different outfit, appearance, and tone, replaced the actor. The substitution was not noticed by a full half of the participants.
The experiment was one of the first to explain the "switch blindness" effect, which demonstrates just how selective we are about what we draw in from any particular visual environment— and it seems we rely substantially more than we might expect on memory and pattern recognition upon.
It's hard to delay gratification— but when we do, we're more effective.

A famous late 1960s Stanford experiment tested the ability of pre-school kids to resist the lure of instant gratification— and gave some powerful insights into willpower and self-discipline. In the study, four-year-olds were put in a space on their own with a marshmallow on a plate in front of them and told they could either enjoy the candy immediately or if they waited until the scientist returned 15 minutes later, they might have two marshmallows.

While most kids said they were going to wait, they often struggled to resist and then gave in, eating the treat before the researcher came back, reports TIME. The kids who managed to hold off for the entire 15 minutes generally used techniques for denial, such as turning away and shielding their faces. The consequences of the behavior of the children are significant: those who were able to delay gratification were far less likely to be obese or to have drug addiction and behavioral problems by the time they were adolescents, and later in life were more successful.

We can experience deeply conflicting moral impulses.

A prominent 1961 experiment by Yale psychologist Stanley Milgram (rather alarmingly) measured how far individuals would go to obedience to figures of authority if asked to hurt others, and the strong internal conflict between personal morals and the obligation to follow figures of authority.
Milgram wanted to experiment to provide insight into how, during the Holocaust, Nazi war criminals could have perpetuated unspeakable acts. To do so, he tested a pair of people, one deemed the "instructor" and the other deemed the "learner." The teacher was told to deliver electrical shocks to the learner (who was supposed to be seated in another room but wasn't shocked) whenever they had wrong questions. Milgram then played tapes that made it sound like the learner was in distress, and if the subject "teacher" expressed a desire to leave, he was prodded by the experimenter to proceed.
65% of participants received an intense, final 450-volt shock (labeled "XXX") during the first test, although many were noticeably nervous and unhappy about doing so.

While the research has traditionally been seen as a sign of blind obedience to authority, it has recently been revisited by Scientific American, suggesting that the findings are more suggestive of deep moral disagreement. "Human moral essence requires a tendency to be empathetic, kind and descent towards our fellow relatives and group members, plus a tendency to be xenophobic, cruel and evil towards tribal others," wrote columnist Michael Shermer. "Shock tests show not blind obedience, but contradictory behavioral impulses that exist deep inside." Recently, some critics criticized Milgram's methods, and one analyst noted that Yale experiment reports indicated that 60 percent of participants reportedly disobeyed orders to deliver the highest-dose shock.

Through energy, they are easily corrupted.

There is a psychological reason behind the fact that often, those in control behave with a sense of entitlement and resentment towards others. A study published in Psychological Review in 2003 put students in groups of three together to write a short paper. Two students were instructed to write the paper, while the other was instructed to assess the paper and determine how much each student would be paid. A scientist held a tray of five cookies amid their study. Although the last cookie has generally never been eaten, the "boss" almost always ate the fourth cookie—and sloppily ate it, open the mouth.

"As scientists empower people in scientific experiments, they are more likely to physically touch others in potentially inappropriate ways, chat more overtly, make provocative decisions and plays, make first concessions in deals, speak their minds, and eat cookies like the Cookie Monster, with crumbs all over their chins and necks.

We seek out loyalty to social groups and are easily drawn to intergroup conflict.

This classic experiment in social psychology in the 1950s shed light on the possible psychological basis of why social groups and countries are in conflict with each other— and how they can learn to cooperate again.
Study leader Muzafer Sherif took two teams of 11 boys (all 11 years old) to Robbers Cave State Park in Oklahoma for "summer camp." The groups (named "Eagles" and "Rattlers") spent a week apart, having fun and bonding with each other, without knowledge of the other group's presence. After actually combining the two teams, the boys started calling each other names, and when they started competing in different games, there was more tension, and gradually the groups refused to eat together.
Sherif planned interventions in the next step of the research to try and resolve the boys by making them enjoy recreational activities together (which was unsuccessful) and then helping them solve a problem together, which eventually began to alleviate the tension.
We need to be satisfied with one thing.

The 75-year Harvard Grant study— one of the most comprehensive longitudinal studies ever conducted — was followed for 75 years by 268 male Harvard undergraduates from the 1938-1940 classes (now well into their 90s), collecting data on various aspects of their lives regularly. The end of the universe? Loving matters, at least in deciding long-term happiness and satisfaction of life.

The long-time director of the experiment, psychologist George Vaillant, told The Huffington Post that there are two foundations of happiness: "One is love. The other is finding a way to cope with a life that does not drive love away." For example, one person began the study with the lowest rating for future stability of all participants and had attempted suicide before. But he's one of the happiest at the end of his life. What's the reason? As Vaillant explains, "He's been looking for love for his life."

We thrive when we have strong self-esteem and social status.

According to the infamous analysis of Oscar winners, gaining fame and success is not just an ego boost— it could also be a path to longevity. Researchers at the Sunnybrook and Women's College, Health Sciences Center in Toronto, found that Academy Award-winning actors and directors tend to live longer than those nominated but lost, with winning actors and actresses surviving their lost peers by almost four years.

We are always trying to justify our experiences and make sense to us.

Anyone who has taken a freshmen Psych 101 course is familiar with cognitive dissonance, a concept that is focused on disharmonious and mutually contradictory assumptions which human beings have a natural propensity to escape emotional confrontation. Psychologist Leon Festinger asked participants to perform a series of dull tasks for an hour, such as turning pegs in a wooden knob, in a frequently cited experiment in 1959. They were then paid either $1 or $20 to claim that the assignment was very important to a "waiting investigator" (aka a researcher).

Those paying to cheat for $1 found the activities more fun than those paid for $20. Their ending? Those who were paying more believed they had enough reason to perform the rote task for an hour, but those who were paid just $1 felt the need to explain the time they spent (and reduce the level of dissonance in their beliefs and behavior) by saying the exercise was enjoyable. In other words, they usually say lies to make the world look more rational, more harmonious.

How To Study Human Behavior

Many people are fascinated by the behavior of people. Why are we doing the way we do? How do we affect and quantify our behavior? And why is it so difficult to change behavior? In this blog post, we describe several theories of behavior as well as different ways of measuring human behavior. Finally, they are addressing research fields in which human behavior, such as health care, education, and consumer research, play a central role.

Behavioral Perspectives: It is the environment Influenced by prominent thinkers such as John B. Watson and B.F. Around 1920 and 1950, Skinner, behavioral psychology became popular. Behaviorism provides a systematic way to study human behavior with its focus on observable behavior rather than mental states.

Behaviorists believe that behavior is learned through contact with our environment and that through repetition, all actions are acquired. Classical and operational conditioning are two key principles used in modern behavior.

Something new is combined with something that occurs naturally in classical conditioning. The new stimulus, after a while, causes the same response as the initial stimulus, leading to a new connection. A well-known example of this principle can be found in research by Ivan Pavlov.

What is modern conditioning?

Pavlov mixed the ringing of a bell (new stimulus) with the appearance of food (naturally occurring stimulus) in his experiments with animals. Eventually, when the dogs heard the bell, even when no food was presented (new association), they started salivating. And behold, the new behavior is being learned.

What is the disposition of the operator?

The second principle of learning, operant conditioning, describes how consequences shape our behavior. In particular, it states that reward and punishment can affect the likelihood that behaviors will occur again.

Talk about how you reward a kid when she eats her food, or how if she's disrespectful to her dad, you could take away a favorite toy. You owe her a penalty for her actions in both situations.

Chances are, next time, she's going to eat her vegetables and think twice about teasing her brother.

The way human behavior is shaped is explained by these methods. Critics argue, however, that behaviorism does not take into consideration important factors such as free will, social causes, and other training forms. We will discuss two other hypotheses of behavior in the next section.

Social learning philosophy: it is many individuals that the concept of social learning was introduced by Albert Bandura in the 1970s, who argued that conditioning alone could not compensate for all actions. Social learning theory suggests that people learn from observing others at their core.

Such perceptual learning happens not only when looking at another person, but also when listening to action explanations and observing visual models. This offers us many learning opportunities from very early on.

Importantly, the theory of social learning emphasizes that mental states, such as motivation or thoughts, also influence behavior.

Another difference with behaviorism is that observer learning does not necessarily result in permanent changes in behavior. In other words, without showing new behaviors, people might learn new information.

So far, through experience and observation, we have discovered that human behavior can be influenced. Relational Frame Theory describes a third method of learning behavior.

Why is changing behavior difficult?

As you may know from personal experience, it can be difficult to change actions. Maybe you've tried to do more exercise or eat healthier foods, to get back to your old habits a week later.

Why is it so difficult to change behavior? And what can you do to be successful anyway.

First, it is important to know that subconscious mechanisms control about 95% of our actions. To be mindful of all our actions, it would simply take too much mental energy. Therefore, then, most of it is part of our routines, routines.

Second, behavioralism has taught us that our actions are influenced by the world through interactions and outcomes. So let's look at the implications of behavior that we want to change.

Think you want to work out more often to return to our previous example. What are the implications of this behavior? More power, cleaner skin, slimmer body. Sounds good. But you need to work out, sweat, and miss cozy sofa hours to get there.

Do you notice the difference, particularly in their timing, between these consequences? The unpleasant consequences come immediately, while for weeks or even months, you have to persevere until you experience the pleasant consequences of your behavior.

If the consequences determine our actions, it is not shocking that over the long-term, theoretical ones, the immediate, tangible incentives prevail. And if we don't know about 95% of our behaviors, how can we expect them to change? Fortunately, we can also take advantage of these principles.

Behavioral shift

A powerful way is through pattern piling to make use of our unconscious habits. It means you're taking an established pattern and then applying to it a new behavior. Of starters, when you forget to take your medication regularly, you'll' frame' this action on top of a routine you've already perfected, like morning brushing your teeth.

You are more likely to stick to it by making a new action part of an established routine. The beauty of it is that once a new behavior has become a habit of itself, you can stack on new behaviors.

The power of consequences You can also harness the power of consequences by creating ways to make your desired behavior's short-term consequences more positive while making the short-term consequences of procrastination more expensive.

For example, every time you eat a healthy meal, you can reward yourself. It can make a difference just by praising yourself for every step in the right direction, as it can actively imagine the long-term benefits of your behavior. And if you want to make procrastination's consequences more expensive, you can try to team up with a buddy, make your intentions public, or make a costly bet on your behavior.

Change your environment

You can take another important step to change your environment. If your tv is on and your sportswear is in the loft, lounging on the sofa is much better than continuing your workout. Then, unplug the television and keep in view, all you need to start exercise.

Principles such as these are also used in behavioral (cognitive) therapy. Behaviors, including anxiety, depression, addictions or other mental disorders, were discussed and gradually changed with the help of a therapist. Accurate measurements and ongoing behavioral research are essential to provide people with the best possible care.

Qualitative versus Quantitative Research

Many sorts of research tools are available to test human behavior. Such methods can be separated into qualitative and quantitative measures.

What is a qualitative investigation?

Through researching underlying reasons, beliefs, and motives, empirical tests help scientists understand human behavior at a deeper level. In understanding the context of phenomena and how they affect individuals and groups, they are particularly helpful. The specifics are all about it. It's about understanding' why' and' how' people are acting as they do.

Tools for assessing qualitative data

The sample size is typically small in this type of research, as it is highly labor-intensive. For example, techniques for assessing qualitative data include in-depth interviews, focus group surveys, findings, and unstructured questionnaires with open-ended questions. Qualitative research is preferably carried out in a natural setting.

What is working in qualitative terms?

Quantitative measurements, on the other hand, are used to calculate attitudes, beliefs, data, habits, and other specified variables–and to generalize outcomes from a larger sample population. Used to answer questions like "How many?" "How often, how often?" "How much, how much?" Responses of which are represented by numbers. The data collected can be interpreted systematically. Methods for gathering these data include, for instance, interviews, standardized questionnaires, or web polls, using close-ended questions.

Combining qualitative and quantitative data Discovering the truth is the overall purpose of research. Yet "you're only guessing without good data." Combining qualitative data with quantitative data will provide investigators with in-depth information on certain behavior and different aspects of that behavior. The two different approaches complement each other while mitigating each other's shortcomings.

Observation

Observations perform a very important part of studying human behavior.

What better way to tell the behavior of somebody than to observe that person? How does the participant of your experiment communicate with a baby, a client, or a computer?

Observational research

Observational research is typically conducted in the home, workplace, or specially designed observation laboratory. Unobtrusively, the best way to observe one's true behavior. You can watch every move of your subject with a one-way mirror without being physically present in the room. By using The Observer XT, all activities of interest can be annotated and interpreted, allowing contextual data measurable.

Visual recordings are a good way to study human behavior, as well. Using recording widens the reach of any research project considerably. Image recording helps you to render frame-accurate action explanations. Vision is the ideal solution for high-quality video and audio recording in multiple rooms and offers the required video material to gain insight into procedures, human performance, and interaction.

Physiological measures

While your test participant may seem calm, a significant amount of stress may be concealed from him or her. You can combine behavioral coding with acquired physiological measurements with a data acquisition system to reveal this level of stress.

While collecting observational data, this allows you to simultaneously acquire physiological data such as EEG, ECG, EMG, blood pressure, skin behavior, and facial expressions. For example, skin conductance is a technique used as an indicator of emotional and physiological arousal to measure the skin's electrical conductance. EEG enables neural activation to be included during a study, while FaceReader detects the emotion of the face. These measurements allow studying the interplay between physiology and behavior, which is caused by an external event.

Implicit measures

While questionnaires may be useful to capture opinions, traits of personality, or (mental) health issues, they also have some limitations.

Another important issue is that in their responses, people can be biased. We tend to give socially desirable responses, we are affected by an experimental environment, and we respond in a certain way to all questions (usually intense and negative, often' yes' or' no').

We don't always understand what we're doing, doing, or doing. Around 95% of our action is subconscious and automatic, as we mentioned earlier in this article. We may be able to escape any knowledge about ourselves.

Studies have built methods to collect our subconscious thoughts, feelings, and actions with these shortcomings in mind. Such implicit assessments demand that individuals respond to different stimuli very rapidly. Reaction time variations reflect how you think about something.

Mental disorders In the prevention and treatment of mental disorders, understanding human nature is important.

Mental disorders are defined as a mixture of anomalous thoughts, emotions, and behaviors. Millions of people worldwide are suffering from disorders such as depression, addiction, anxiety, and dementia.

Besides a host of emotional and behavioral effects, mentally disordered individuals also often have problems in school, employment, and family life.

Understanding mental disorders

Testing plays an important role in the further explanation of these conditions with this variety of symptoms and contributing factors.

Learning & Training

Education is about acquiring knowledge of students about reality, things, morals, views, basic ideas, ideals, etc. On the other hand, rather than just learning about something, education is a way to develop skills. Education is based on practical application, requiring practical experience, or helping people to implement a new program, develop a particular skill, or further their potential in something.

Education and training may take place in a wide range of fields and many different settings, such as schools and labs for expertise. In a safe and controlled environment, theory can be put into practice.

Conclusion

Understanding human nature by connecting the elements Because dreams always come in the form of symbols, Brian's dream of losing the car was only a reflection of his fear of losing his status. In other words, the vision meant Brian was worried about losing his rank and reputation! (See what your dream means) Because the subconscious mind thinks using symbols and because logic is to some extent ignored during its operation, the mind of Brian forced him to develop that obsessive-compulsive disorder because he was so concerned about the threat of losing his status. In other words, Brian developed the disorder because he was too afraid to lose his status and checking if the car was locked or not reflected his fear of losing his car if he became poor.

This is how human behavior can be interpreted in trying to understand human behavior, by analyzing all the objects in the process, never investigate a single item.

If a woman is scared of cats, then you should try to look at other aspects of her life instead of automatically thinking that traumatic experience with cats happened to her when she was young.

Could this cat's fear to represent her other women's terror?

Will her low self-esteem render her exposed in her subconscious mind to the presence of other people symbolized in the form of cats?

Of course, I'm not telling you to research the previous examples by saying that every person who has such a condition is afraid to lose his rank or that every woman who is scared of cats has low self-esteem, but instead, I'm asking you to look deeper and understand the human actions better.

Why Critical Thinking Is Important

Better critical thinking skills can bring about a big positive change in your life by improving the quality of your thoughts and decisions. Know how to do that.

It's not an exaggeration to say that the quality of your life depends largely on the value of your choices.

Surprisingly, every day, the average person makes 35,000 conscious decisions!

Imagine how much better life could be if there were a tool to make the best decisions you can take day in and day out?

Okay, there's critical thinking, and it's called that.

Training to develop critical thinking skills can have a profound impact on almost every aspect of your life.

Major Benefits of Developing Critical Thinking

Whether or not you think critically in just about every area of your life can make the difference between success and failure.

The human brains are flawed, vulnerable to irrationality, exaggeration, bias, or intellectual discrimination.

Cognitive biases are irrational, thinking systematic patterns.

Although the number of cognitive biases varies, Wikipedia lists more than 150 of them, for example!

Some of the most popular biases include catastrophic thinking, the bias in confirmation, and fear of missing out (FOMO).

Critical thinking will help you move beyond emotional thinking limits.

Here are some critical thinking's most important benefits for your life.

1. Critical Thinking Is a Key to Career Success

Critical thinking is an absolute must in most fields.

Critical thinking must be used frequently by lawyers, analysts, accountants, doctors, engineers, reporters, and scientists of all kinds.

Yet critical thinking is a skill set that in a growing number of careers is becoming increasingly valuable.

Critical thinking can help you in any profession where you need to analyze information, solve problems in a systematic manner, generate innovative solutions, plan strategically, think creatively, or present your work or ideas to others in a way that is easy to understand.

Critical thinking and complex problem solving are the two most in-demand qualities employers are looking for, according to the World Economic Forum.

Critical thinking is called a soft skill and strategic ability — a central trait needed to succeed in the workforce.

Certain soft skills include problem-solving, imagination, ability to communicate and present, and electronic literacy.

Critical thinking can also help you develop the remaining soft skills.

Developing your critical thinking will help you get a job, as many candidates can ask your questions about jobs or even give you a sample of how well you can think objectively.

It can also motivate you to excel consistently in your life, as being a critical thinker is a strong long-term success indicator.

2. Critical Thinkers Make Better Decisions

You make thousands of choices every day.
Most of them are made by your subconscious, and some of them, like the shoes to wear today, don't need much thought.
But the most important decisions you make can be difficult and require a lot of thinking, such as when or when to switch careers, move to a new town, buy a house, get married or have children.
You may need to make decisions at work that can change the course of your life or other people's lives.
Critical thinking helps you deal with the daily problems that arise.
It promotes independent thinking and strengthens your internal "BS detector." It helps you make sense of the abundance of available data and information, making you a smarter consumer less likely to fall for advertising, peer pressure, or scams.

3. Critical Thinking Can Make You Happier

Knowing and understanding yourself is a path to happiness that is undervalued.

We have already seen how the quality of your life depends largely on the value of your decisions, but the quality of your thinking is just as important.

Critical thinking is a good tool to help you understand yourself better and learn how to improve your thoughts.

Critical thinking can be used to free yourself from cognitive biases, cynical thoughts, or restricting the values that hold you back in any area of your life.

Critical thinking will help you analyze your strengths and weaknesses, and you know what to give and where to apply changes.

Critical thinking will make it possible for you to articulate your feelings, ideas, and beliefs more.

Better communication leads to less anger and is harder for others to understand.

It fosters creativity and thinking out of the box that can be applied to any area of your life.

Critical thinking provides you with a system on which you can concentrate, making decisions less difficult.

It can boost your trust as you and those around you are confident that your views are well thought out.

You are discouraged from jumping to conclusions by critical thinking.

If debates get hot, you can count on being the voice of reason.

You will also be better able to detect when others are disingenuous, do not have your best interests at heart, or try to exploit or manipulate you.

6. Critical Thinking Makes You a Better, More Informed Citizen

"An educated citizenry is a vital requirement for our survival as a free person." This quote was incorrectly attributed to Thomas Jefferson, but his words of wisdom are more relevant than ever, regardless of the source.

Critical thinkers can see both sides of any problem and are more likely to find bipartisan solutions.

Propaganda is less likely to sway them, or they are swept up in mass hysteria.

We are in a better position when they see it to spot fake news.

4. Critical Thinking Ensures Your Opinions Are Well-Informed

More information is available to us than ever before.

Amazingly, in the past two years, more data has been created than in human history as a whole.

Critical thinking will allow you to work out the noise.

American politician, sociologist, and diplomat Daniel Patrick Moynihan once said, "You have the right to your opinion. But you do not have the right to your facts. "Critical thinking means that your conclusions are well educated and founded on the latest facts available.

5. Critical Thinking Improves Relationships

You may be concerned that critical thinking will make you a Spock-like character that is not very good in relationships.

But the opposite is true, in truth.

Using critical thinking makes you more open-minded and more capable of understanding the points of view of others.

Critical thinkers are more empathic and able to get along with different types of people.

Critical thinking is considered to incorporate a wide range of subjects and to develop a wide range of intellectual skills. One might say it's a cross-curricular support for the body, and to stay healthy, the mind must be worked just like a muscle.

Critical thinking, among many other things, promotes the development of things like:

- ➢ Reasoning skills
- ➢ Analytical thinking
- ➢ Evaluative skills
- ➢ Logical thinking
- ➢ Organizational and planning skills
- ➢ Language skills
- ➢ Self-reflective skills
- ➢ Observational skills
- ➢ Open-mindedness
- ➢ Creative visualization techniques
- ➢ Questioning skills
- ➢ Decision making

This list could easily be expanded to include other skills, but this gives one an idea of just what is being developed.

How to Make Better Decisions

You understand what is involved in problem-solving and critical thinking. These ideas can make you a better problem solver at school or in your personal life when faced with challenges, not only will you learn how to make better business decisions. Also, we will provide you with amazing online tools, videos, and resources throughout this guide to help you keep learning how to make better decisions about your daily activities.
The Importance of Creative Problem Solving in Business and Life
One of the leadership skills that successful business people and people in business are supposed to have is the importance of creative problem-solving in business and life problem solving, yet many fail with the easiest of decisions. What makes it so easy for one person to solve everyday problems and fail for the next?

The truth is, even experienced decision-makers hone their creative problem-solving skills continuously and perfectly. And there's a lot of compelling reasons to do that. Not only do those who make better decisions have more job opportunities, get promoted more often, and increase the productivity of their careers, but they are more satisfied in particular. In a recent study by the University of Chicago School of Business, research found that satisfaction is more dependent on decision-making incentives (i.e., freedom) than on money or relationships. This means that decision-making ability leads to more and better chances of success, which improves your quality of life. In other words, the better you're a decision-maker, the healthier and better you're going to be.

This theory runs counter to what many business leaders believe–that what makes you successful is what you learn and who you meet. In reality, the key to success is how you interpret and solve problems.

Luckily, problem-solving and decision-making are abilities that can be reinforced, learned, and perfected. You can see problems earlier and make decisions faster by learning specific problem solving and decision-making techniques. This helps you to make more comfortable choices in your career and allows you greater control over satisfaction and efficiency in every part of your life.

Critical Thinking in the Decision Making Process

You understand what is involved in problem-solving and critical thinking. These ideas can make you a better problem solver at school or in your personal life when faced with challenges, not only will you learn how to make better business decisions. Also, we will provide you with amazing online tools, videos, and resources throughout this guide to help you keep learning how to make better decisions about your daily activities.

Critical thinking is the practice of collecting, analyzing, and evaluating information methodically. It is one of the most important parts of the problem-solving and decision-making process, as it is the task of thinking clearly about choices that will lead to a final choice. While decision-making is the process that leads to actionable conclusions, the element that defines whether the choice is sound is critical thinking. Think about it this way: if the vehicle that takes your company to its targets is to solve problems, the fuel is critical thinking skills.

Although people have been thinking critically since a stone tool was picked up by the first Homo Habilis, critical thinking as a process has only become one of the most valuable business skills of the last century. In his 1938 essay, Logic: The Concept of Inquiry, John F. Dewey, founder of the Dewey library system and a well-known academic theorist, started to emphasize the importance of developing critical thinking skills.

Critical thinking and decision-making since that time have been synonymous with business skills that corporate leaders expect. Still, many people don't understand the underlying concepts that make an effective process of critical thinking. All critical thinking is based on four key structures:

Logic–the ability of an individual to see direct cause-effect relationships. This is one of the most important decision-making skills because reasoning makes accurate forecasts of what kinds of effects a potential solution will have on individuals and processes.

Truth–An event's impartial information. An important part of the problem-solving process is objective and unemotional truth. Good critical reasoning abolishes these stereotypes and draws on existing and recorded data supporting the conclusion.

Context–A list of extenuating conditions or causes that the final solution will or should impact. Critical thinking should take into account the past success of similar solutions, the decision-maker's external or theoretical stresses, and specific investors ' expectations and interests. To participate in a strategic decision-making process, all these external factors must be addressed.

Alternatives–Possible solutions not in use at the moment. Through active critical thinking, the participant should consider new ways to address challenges that meet real-world expectations and are focused on reliable, objective data. This is the case, even if there are no alternative solutions, or if there are unexpected external determinants.

You will become more mindful of personal biases once you know each of these underlying factors and become more interested in the critical thinking process. Furthermore, improving your critical thinking skills will result in faster, more confident, and more productive decision-making. Critical thinking fuel is the secret ingredient that drives the success of your business.

Step Problem Solving Method

Although many have made variants on the 6-step problem-solving technique, in the 1950s Dr. Sidney J. Parnes and Alex Osborn invented the only research-based version of this approach. After working with and observing high-level advertising employees throughout the process of brainstorming and implementation, Parnes and Osborn recognized that creative people are going through several stages as they create, organize, and select good solutions to problems. They published their findings in 1979 under the title, Applied Imagination: Creative Thinking Principles and Procedures.

The 6-Step model, "The Creative Problem Solving (CPS) Method" was called in their original work and included these key segments:

> Objective Search
> Finding the Proof
> Seeing the question
> Getting the Word
> Finding Solution
> Finding acceptance

These six segments were further organized into three key phases of problem-solving: Challenge exploration, Idea generation, and Action Preparedness.

This model also includes elements from the Soft Stage Management (SSM) model, which provides a seven-stage approach to problem-solving. Businesses and organizations around the world have adopted the Yale adaptation and include these four steps of action:

> Define the problem
> Determine the root cause of the problem
> Developing alternative solutions
> Choose a solution to incorporate the solution.

Effective Ways to Enhance Your Problem Solving Skills

Did you ever think of yourself as a solver of problems? I don't feel so. In reality, however, we are always solving problems. And the greater our ability to solve problems, the happier our lives will be.

Problems arise in many forms and shapes. They can be mundane, daily issues, or more complex issues: what to have tonight for dinner?

What a way to get to work?

How can a project be fixed that runs behind schedule?

How to change from an uninspiring job to a career that you love?

You're going to face at least one question every day to solve. But when you know that things are simply decisions, it becomes simpler. Nothing but having to make a decision is' scary' with them.

Whatever job you are in, wherever you live, who your partner is, how many friends you have, your ability to solve problems will be judged. Because of those involved, challenges are similar hassles. And people don't like to have trouble. The more problems you can fix, the less difficult the whole matter, the happier people are with you. Everybody's winning.

Why Are Problem Solving Skills Important?

The problem is difficult to understand, accomplish, or deal with. It may be a mission, a circumstance, or even a person. Problem-solving requires finding the best solutions to problems using techniques and skills.

Problem-solving is important because, in our lives, we all have to make decisions and answer questions. Good solvers for challenges are amazing people like Eleanor Roosevelt, Steve Jobs, Mahatma Gandhi, and Martin Luther King Jr. Good parents, teachers, nurses, and waiters must all also be good at solving all kinds of problems.

Skills solving problems are in our daily lives.

How to develop problem-solving skills Many people think you need to be very intelligent to be a good problem solver, but that's not true.

To be a problem solver, you don't have to be super smart, and you need to learn.

You will be able to come up with great solutions if you know the different steps to solve a problem.

1. Focus on the Solution, Not the Problem

Neuroscientists have demonstrated that if you focus on the problem, your brain can't find solutions. This is because when you focus on the problem, you feed' negativity' effectively, which in turn activates negative brain emotions. Potential solutions obstruct these feelings.

I'm not saying you're going to' know the problem,' try to stay cool. It helps to recognize the problem first; and then move your focus to a solution-oriented mindset where you stay fixed on what the' answer' might be, instead of lingering on' what went wrong' and' who's fault it's.'

2. Adapt 5 Whys to define the problem clearly

5 Whys to help you get to the root of a problem is a problem-solving framework.

You can delve into the root cause of a dilemma by constantly asking the question "why" on a topic, and that's how you can find the best solution to deal with the root issue once and for all. And it can go further than just five times asking why.

For example: if "too late to work" is the issue...

> Why am I working late?

I always click on the snooze button to go to sleep.

> Why should I go to sleep?

In the night, I felt so drained.

> Why am I feeling tired in the morning?

I slept before late that night; that's why.

> Why was I late sleeping?

After drinking coffee, I wasn't sleepy, and I was scrolling my Facebook feed, and I couldn't stop somehow.

> How have I been drinking coffee?

Because in the afternoon I was too sleepy at work, the night before I didn't sleep enough.

So you see, if you haven't tried to dig out the root of the issue, you might just set a few more alarms and beep it every five minutes in the morning. But in fact, the problem you need to solve is to stop surfing on Facebook endlessly at night, so you'll feel more energetic during the daytime, and you won't even need coffee.

3. Simplify Things

As human beings, and they prefer to complicate things more than they need to be! By generalizing it, try to simplify the problem.
Delete all the information and stick to the basics. Try to find a very simple, obvious solution–the findings could shock you!

4. List out as Many Solutions as Possible

Try to come up with' ALL POSSIBLE SOLUTIONS'–even though at first they look ridiculous. To boost creative thinking, it's important to keep an open mind that can trigger potential solutions.
Coming from 10 years in the corporate advertising industry,' No idea is a bad idea' is drummed into you, and this helps creative thinking in brainstorms and other problem-solving techniques.

Whatever you do, don't get ridiculed about' stupid solutions' because it's often the crazy ideas that trigger other more viable solutions.

5. Think Laterally

Shift your mind course by looking laterally. Look at the saying, try changing your attitude, and looking at things in a new way. You can try to flip around your target and look for a polar opposite solution!

A new and creative strategy, even if it sounds crazy, typically triggers a fresh response.

6. Use Language That Creates Possibility

Lead the thought with phrases such as' what if...' and' imagines if...' that enable our brains to think creatively and promote solutions.

The Bottom Line

Once you begin to adapt my suggestions, nothing is frightening about a problem.

Attempt not to see things as' scary' stuff! If you're talking about what the real problem is, it's just suggestions about your current situation.

Every problem tells you that something doesn't work at the moment and you need to find a new way around it.

Therefore, try to approach issues neutrally–without any judgment. We are focusing on describing a problem, keeping calm and not making things too complicated.

Negative Self-Talk: Ways To Silence Your Inner Critic

Is it half-empty and half-full of your glass? How you respond to this age-old question about positive thinking may reflect your life outlook, your attitude towards yourself, and whether you are optimistic or pessimistic — and may even affect your health.

Yes, some studies show that characteristics of personality, such as enthusiasm and pessimism, can influence some aspects of your well-being and well-being. A key part of good stress management is the positive thinking that usually comes to motivation. And there are many health benefits associated with effective stress management. You can learn positive thinking skills when you happen to be cynical, do not despair.

What's Self-Talk Negative?

We're spending so much time thinking we're not good enough, intelligent enough, creative enough, and slim enough.

We're implying we don't deserve the things we want.

Or that the things they want to have and witness are never going to happen, and even if they do, they are going to be frustrating.

If we think something is possible, we will make an effort to achieve it more likely. We're not even going to bother trying because we think it's unlikely.

If we think we're a good person who's worth living a life we love, we're going to create that life. But if we think we're underserved or not capable enough, we're going to sabotage our efforts without realizing it.

Studies show that your thoughts also affect your body physically. Take, for example, polygraph tests (commonly known as lie detector tests).

We demonstrate that your emotions directly affect your blood pressure, muscle tension, temperature, respiration speed, heart rate, and how much you sweat your palms. These are some very important physical reactions to our thoughts!

Effects of Negative Self-Talk

If you experience the effects of negative thoughts, such as feelings that produce the emotional states of terror, rage, depression, remorse, embarrassment, and regret:

> The muscles in your body are stronger, literally.

> The stress levels are rising.
> Changes in your biochemistry and hormone levels, and you may even have gastrointestinal or digestive problems with other physical symptoms.

Studies also show that negative people appear to be more anxious and less happy with life in general.

Through comparison, you fill your brain with endorphins when you have positive thoughts, which allows you to calm so that you are more alert and focused.

Not only that, while reducing physical pain, positive thinking increases your experience of pleasure.

And as a result, you are much more likely to be positive, ambitious, so inspired to attain your goals.

How to Stop Negative Self-Talk

But for some men, it's easier to say than done to switch their negative thoughts to positive ones.

Most men, like themselves, have a lifelong habit of seeing the negative in all things. We try to justify their cynicism by pointing out all the negative things that are happening in the world and claiming we are "just being rational," but in fact, all they do is undermine themselves mentally.

The good news is. You're in control of your feelings because you're their source!

That means you can learn to choose consciously to replace your negative thoughts with positive thoughts that will improve your life. Not all negative thoughts are the product of running wild with your inner critic.

There are other forms of negative thinking that you can build a healthier, more productive, and more fulfilling life if you can learn to recognize them and combat them.

Negative self-talk examples–And how to overcome them

I want to share five of the main types of negative thinking –so when they happen you can recognize them and then consciously choose to replace them with something more positive.

1. "Always or Never" Thinking

That's when you're just wondering, never, every time, everyone, nothing, and so on.

For example, thoughts like, "I'm not going to get a raise," or, "Nobody thinks about me," or, "I'm just screwing up, no matter what." Not only is this kind of thinking detrimental to your well-being, but it's also not focused. It's not true that you don't care for NO ONE, or you're never going to get a rise.

Okay, if you never do the job you need to get a bonus, that last one might be real. Yet then you're the one who causes the scenario. Which means you can change it.

It's not a given absolute.

2. "Focusing on the Negative" Feeling

It is when you're so busy looking at the world's bad things, you can't see the good things.

But the fact is not all life is bad, just as it's not all good. It's both a combination. For pretty much all, there's a positive side and a negative side.

And since you can choose what to focus on, why not focus on the positive?

I promise you that if you do, it will have a much better impact on your life and health.

3. Catastrophic Predicting

This is when you imagine the worst outcome in any situation and are convinced of its inevitability–usually without any real facts to support it.

A good example of this would be that you are beginning to imagine that you will be laid off from work, or that North Korea will send a nuclear missile and blow up Los Angeles, even if there is no concrete evidence to support your prediction.

Although the worst-case scenario seldom exists, you're behaving like it's just a matter of time or encouraging your thoughts and actions to control.

The reality is we never know what the future holds–and history shows the rare occurrence of worst-case scenarios. So why think about something that hasn't happened yet, and is probably never going to happen?

You're probably better off just concentrating on what's going on right now and reflecting on it–like the task at hand.

4. Mind Reading A sly one is the fourth form of negative thinking.

This is when you convince yourself that you know what someone else is doing–and that's always negative.

Are you ever arguing with someone in your head?

You imagine them saying all kinds of awful things that frustrate you and make you angry and injure you or make you feel ashamed?

That's mind reading... you don't know what that person is thinking. But you're asking yourself to do it–and you're letting this false belief affect your friendships adversely.

Note, you certainly aren't psychic. The only way you can know what someone else thinks is to ask them and have an honest talk about it. That's also how you form relationships that are deeper and more meaningful.

5. Guilt Tripping

Guilt-tripping is all that makes you feel embarrassed and humiliated when you reflect on all the bad things you've ever done, and you allow that to determine your view of who you are.

You say you're a failure and a bad person, and you don't deserve to feel good or gain the happiness you're looking forward to.

And so, before you even begin, you give up.

It's been observed that people wasting their entire lives because of their feelings of guilt for something they had done decades ago – divorce, loss of family because of their alcohol or drug addiction, traffic accidents, failure of troops under their control in combat, incarceration, and insistence that someone else's death and suicide could have been avoided if they had acted differently.

The truth is, EVERYONE has done things that they regret, including me.

You're not supposed to let that define you.

You've done a lot of great things in your life as well.

When you concentrate on the good things and continue to see yourself as a fundamentally good person who has made many mistakes but is also able to accomplish great things, you will once again open yourself to a future of limitless opportunity.

Stop today's Poor Self-Talk!

Start listening to how you're speaking about yourself and how you're talking to others.

Are you focusing on the negative and assuming the worst?

Should you break yourself down constantly?

Would you feel "always or never" in spite of this?

Would you suppose you know what others feel without having to check it out?

Each time you find yourself thinking a negative thought, say the words quietly and softly, "Cancel-Cancel" and then change it deliberately instead of a positive thought.

Steps to Developing Critical Thinking Skills

Would you react to circumstances that are based on your emotions or biases? Looking for ways to communicate better with those around you? Would you like to do more in your career?

You can develop your ability to make rational, meaningful decisions and conclusions by incorporating critical thinking skills. The conclusions can often be one-sided without these capabilities. Criticism may sound like a personal attack on your personality rather than an invitation for discussion and constructive interaction.

Let's look at how to improve critical thinking skills so you can take the tools you need to set aside strong emotions and make smart decisions in any situation:

1. Become a Self-Critic

In developing critical thinking skills, the very first and most important step is to become a critic of your thoughts and actions. You can't grow without self-reflection.

By asking yourself why you believe something, you can break down your thoughts. You need to justify your feelings when you do this by logically analyzing your answer and providing a clear argument that reinforces what you believe. You can stand back and observe how you react to circumstances as you focus on yourself.

During self-reflection, important questions to ask include: Why do I believe this? May I think of examples that proved to be true or false in my life? Am I emotionally attached to that idea? What's the reason?

The identification of your talents, shortcomings, personal preferences, and prejudices is another component of becoming a self-critic. You can understand why you are approaching certain situations with certain perspectives when you know this information. When you are aware of your point of view, if necessary, you can go beyond it.

2. Listen Actively

It is almost impossible to think and listen at the same time. To become a critical thinker, you need to be able to listen to the ideas, arguments, and criticisms of others while they are speaking without thinking about your answer.

If you don't take the time to listen, you can't properly comprehend the knowledge that someone is trying to convey.

Hearing enables you to feel empathy. You can understand their stories, their struggles, their passions, and their ideas when you hear someone else's perspective. Listening actively enables you to understand what somebody is trying to tell you because it pushes the conversation until all parties can reiterate what the others are trying to say.

3. Analytic Knowledge

At all times, no one considers objectively. Your joy, rage, sorrow, or other feelings are too strong sometimes. Sometimes, you are unable to concentrate on the core issue at hand.

Critical thinking demands that the data before you are thoroughly examined, whether it is knowledge in your head or information shared by others. First, evaluate what's being said to analyze information and make sure you understand it clearly. You can then dissect and evaluate all arguments, including your own.

4. Communicate Nonviolently

If you are unable to communicate in a peaceful, productive manner, critical thinking is not much help. You must first understand valid logic when responding to and evaluating arguments. You then need to interact productively with the other people involved.

Compassion, reflection, and cooperation are the pillars of constructive interaction. If you approach a situation with empathy, instead of a protective, you approach it with a calm attitude. If you observe, without bias or personal commitment, you will observe your claims and others. Teamwork occurs when everyone approaches the system with a caring, open-minded approach to solving the problem.

5. Create Foresight

Foresight is the ability to predict a decision's future impact that is critical to success in all aspects of your life. For starters, your plan to see what the job outlook is and what the area is like when you go elsewhere.

Likewise, it is prudent to analyze the effect of that decision if you are moving a company. Is it going to be too far from some of your talented staff to travel? Are you going to lose customers? What are you going to gain?

Before any decision is made, the potential impacts should be carefully weighed.

Do Your Research

All the information that is thrown at us daily can be overwhelming, but it can also be a very powerful tool if you decide to take things into your own hands. Go online to start reading about it if you have a problem to solve, a decision to take, or a view to considering. The more knowledge you have, the more you will be prepared to think about things and find a rational answer to your question.

Why Is Thinking Critically
So Hard?

Educators have long known that attendance at college and even academic success is no guarantee that in all cases a student can graduate a successful thinker. There is a peculiar propensity for systematic analysis to stick to specific examples and categories of concerns. Thus, before starting calculations, a student may have learned to estimate the answer to a math problem as a way to check the accuracy of his answer, but in the chemistry laboratory, the same student calculates the components of a compound without noticing that his estimates are more than 100%. And a student who has learned to reflect on the causes of the American Revolution from both the British and American perspectives does not even think of questioning how the Germans viewed World War II. Why are students capable of thinking critically in one situation, but not in another? The brief answer is: Processes of reasoning are associated with what is being contemplated. Let's explore this in detail by looking at a specific type of critical thinking that has been extensively studied: problem-solving.

Imagine a math class of seventh grade immersed in word issues. How can students answer one problem, but not the next one, even though mathematically, all word problems are the same, that is, they depend on the same knowledge of mathematics? The students typically focus on the scenario described by the word problem (it's surface structure) rather than on the mathematics needed to solve it (its deep structure). So even though students have been taught how to solve a specific type of word problem, students still struggle to apply the solution when the teacher or textbook changes the scenario because they don't recognize that the problems are mathematically the same.

Thinking tends to focus on a problem's "surface structure"

To explain why a problem's surface structure is so confusing and, as a result, how adapting common solutions to new problems is so complicated, let's first consider how you interpret what is being asked when you get a problem. Everything you hear or read is viewed immediately in the light of what you already know about similar topics.

For example, suppose you read these two sentences: "After years of pressure from the film and television industry, the president has lodged a formal complaint with China about what U.S. firms say is copyright infringement, claiming the Chinese government is imposing strict trade restrictions on U.S. entertainment products, even as it turns a blind eye to Chinese firms copying America. For instance, if you read the word "Bush" later, it wouldn't make you think of a small shrub, nor would you ask if it referred to the former president Bush, the rock band, or a term for rural hinterlands. When you hear "corruption," you wouldn't dream about eye-patched swabbies screaming "shiver me timbers!" The mental system is pretending the new data is connected to what you've just talked of. Therefore, the range of possible interpretations of words, phrases, and concepts is greatly limited. The advantage is that understanding goes faster and smoother; the cost is that it is harder to recognize the deep structure of a problem.

The filtering of thoughts that happens when learning (or listening) means you tend to focus on the structure of the surface rather than the underlying structure of the problem. For example, a question like this was seen by four people in one experiment: West High School Band members were hard at work preparing for the annual Homecoming Parade.

They first attempted to march in 12 columns, but Andrew was left alone to lift the tail. The director then told the members of the band to march in eight columns, but Andrew was left alone to march. Andrew was left out even when the unit marched in lines of three. Andrew finally told the band manager in exasperation that they should march in lines of five to cover all the columns. He's got it right. Since there were at least 45 musicians on the field, but less than 200 players, how many students in the West High School Band were there?

The participants had read four issues earlier in the study along with detailed explanations of how to address each, presumably to score them for the quality of the prose. One of the four problems was the number of vegetables to buy from a garden, and it relied on the same type of solution needed to calculate the least common multiple problems for the band. Yet few subjects— only 19 percent— say that the situation with the group was different and they could use the solution to the garden problem. What's the reason?

When a student reads a word problem, given her prior knowledge, her mind interprets the problem as it happened when you read the two phrases about copyrights and China.

The challenge is that the information that seems important applies to the nature of the surface— the reader dredges knowledge about bands, high school, musicians, and so on in this issue. Using the least common multiple, the student is unable to read the question and learn about it in terms of its complex structure. The problem's surface structure is over, but the problem's underlying structure is not. Thus, people don't use the first problem to help them solve the second: the first was about vegetables in a garden in their minds, and the second was about band marchers ' rows.

With deep knowledge, thinking can penetrate beyond surface structure

When knowledge of how to solve a problem has never been applied to concerns of new surface systems, schooling would be inefficient or even futile— but, of course, such a transition is taking place. When and why is complex, five but two factors are particularly relevant to educators: familiar with the deep structure of a problem and the knowledge that a profound structure should be looked for. In turn, I'm going to address each. Knowledge about how to solve it translates well when you are familiar with the deep structure of a problem.

That familiarity may come from long-term, repeated experience with one problem, or with different manifestations of one problem type (i.e., many problems with different surface structures, but the same deep structure). The subject perceives the deep structure as part of the problem description following repeated exposure to either or both. Here's an example: A seeker of gold can discover a cave on a hill close to a beach. He believed that inside the cave there could be many directions so he was scared he might get lost. He did not have a map of the cave, of course; all he had with him were some common items like a torch and a wallet. What could he do to make sure he wasn't lost trying later to get out of the cave? The solution is to carry some sand in your bag and leave a trail as you go, so when you're ready to leave the cave, you can trace your way back. About 75% of American college students thought of this solution — but only 25% of Chinese students solved it.6 The experimenters indicated that Americans solved it because most of them grew up reading Hansel and Gretel's novel, which involves the idea of leaving a trail as you ride to an unidentified place to find your way back. The experimenters also offered participants another puzzle based on a common folk tale in China and reversed the percentage of solvers from each group.

It takes a lot of practice with a problem type before students know it well enough to recognize its deep structure immediately, regardless of the surface structure, as the Americans did for the problem of Hansel and Gretel. In terms of rocks, caves, and gold, American subjects did not think about the problem; they thought about it in terms of finding something to leave a trail. The problem's deep complexity is so well reflected in their minds that when they read the problem, they automatically saw that structure.

The Phases of Critical Thinking

"Learning to think better by improving one's thinking skills" can be defined as critical thinking. Individuals who are critical thinkers use the thinking process to analyze (consider and reflect) and synthesize (piece together) what they have learned or are currently learning. Sadly, a lot of the reasoning of everybody appears to be skewed, imprecise, vague, uninformed, and prejudiced. Critical thinking is needed to improve its quality and value as this becomes severely restrictive.

Critical thinking is necessary within the organizational setting for overcoming problems, making changes, modifications, or adaptations within work structures, methods, and situations solving problems solving situational conflicts and pressing issues, and inventing and implementing new ideas, techniques, and solutions.

The development of critical thinking is a gradual process. This requires: overcoming learning plateaus as well as maintaining a careful eye on the system itself, modifying personal thought patterns, which appear to be a long-range task and considerable time for progress.

It is important to recognize what does not include its basic elements or components in the critical thinking process. Critical thinking is not accomplished by saying something without carefully thinking about it, by guessing what one thinks "should" be done, by memorizing material to analyze, discuss or examine, by doing something just because it has always been done, by believing something because it is what everyone else tends to believe, or by arguing about something when there is no evidence to support the argument.

Critical Thinking

Attributes Critical thinkers embody certain attributes, and these traits help to identify people as "deep thinkers," distinguishing them from more traditional "ordinary thinkers." Critical thinkers tend to be self-disciplined, self-directed, self-monitored and self-correcting thinkers. They raise important or crucial questions and problems and then formulate them clearly and accurately.

Critical thinkers are gathering, compiling, analyzing and assessing relevant information. They come up with sound assumptions, conclusions, and ideas, while they are measured and tested against specific expectations and parameters.

They also maintain an open mind within alternative thinking systems, while continuously recognizing and evaluating their assumptions and reasoning lines. Eventually, critical thinkers effectively communicate with others in looking for and finding answers to issues and problems.

There tend to be six phases of developmental thinking leading to the art of critical thinking being "mastered." Through extensive practice and process applications, individuals can expect to begin to change their thinking habits and eventually change them. Each phase of progress is described below.

- Phase One: The Unenlightened Thinker-Individuals are generally unaware that there are significant issues within their current thinking patterns.
- Phase Two: The Confronted Thinker-Individuals are aware that existing problems within their thinking process are evident or apparent.
- Phase 3: Novice Thinker-individuals seek to facilitate changes to their thought, but without focusing on routine and reliable training.
- Phase Four: Proactive Thinker-Individuals recognize the importance of regular practice to develop their thoughts and strengthen it.
- Phase Five: The Developed Thinker-Individuals continue to develop according to the amount of practice provided to the system.
- Phase Six: Mastery Thinker-individuals become professional and articulate when critical, logical, and evaluative reasoning becomes second nature.

Individuals will progress through these stages only if they accept the fact that there are serious problems with their current processes and thought strategies and can accept the difficulty their reasoning brings to them and make it a point to begin regular practice to refine and strengthen the components and elements of critical thinking.

Critical thinking depends on the clarity of purpose
To develop critical thinking, and it is crucial for individuals to be consistent about the purpose of the mission or the subject at hand, as well as the key issue at stake in this regard.

To achieve this goal, it is essential: to strive to be clear, accurate, accurate and relevant, to practice under-the-surface thinking, to be logical and fair-minded, to apply critical thinking skills to all activities of reading, writing, speaking and listening, and to apply these skills to all aspects of work and life in general.

Questioning: Dead-minded   questions reflect the impetus for critical thinking.

Unfortunately, most people (including managers, leaders, and trainers) do not tend to ask many kinds of questions that stimulate thought. We tend to stick with dead topics such as, "Will this be what is expected from now on?" and, "How are we going to know (or do) this?" and other things that suggest the tendency not to consider outwardly.

The addition, many administrators, leaders, coaches, and facilitators are not themselves creators of in-depth questions and responses of their own making, which helps to create non-critical thinking environments. These individuals are not seriously engaged in thinking through or rethinking through their initiatives, issues, concerns, topics, or instructional concepts and resort to being merely suppliers of the "questions and answers of others." They often end up initiating or responding to some initial concerns or issues that tend to spontaneously surface during a discussion or meeting, without having to go through them. They sometimes tend to apply second-hand information, knowledge or questions that have been passed on, limiting creative evaluations and questioning at a deeper level. They often find themselves referring to authors or others who are considered experts or leaders in their field rather than questioning important issues, ideas, methods, or concerns related to the workplace that need to be examined in depth.

Questioning Through Critical Thinking Keeps the Organization Alive

To the extent that fresh questions are generated and taken seriously, each company remains alive. Such issues are then used as the driving force for improvements to be made and enforced. To think through or reconsider something, individuals within an organization have to ask questions that encourage deeper levels of thinking. Questions specify roles, describe conflicts and communicate concerns. Although, on the other hand, responses frequently signal a complete stop in thought. The thought continues to add value in terms of personal as well as organizational growth and change only when the answers generate further questions.It is important to remember that the individuals within an organization who create and pose difficult and informative questions are the ones who analyze, grow and understand. An organization can be moved forward by simply asking employees to list all the questions they have about an issue, method, or topic, including all the questions generated by their first list of questions. Deep questions, however, drive thoughts that lie beneath the surface of things and force people to deal with complexity.

While purpose questions force individuals to define "their task," information issues force individuals to look at their information source(s) as well as their quality.

Critical Thinking Toward Business Success

Businesses will need to hire employees who can think critically if they want to remain competitive and efficient. Hiring someone with a college degree is not enough. Curious, logical, and strong problem-solvers will have to be new hires. According to industry studies, when assessing job candidates, tactical and critical thinking is the capability most needed by businesses around the world. Critical thinking, problem-solving, decision making, strategic planning, and risk management have also been listed by the U.S. Department of Labor as a core workforce capability. Employers expect that recruits have more than knowledge of textbooks and technical skills and agree that critical thinking is crucial for job performance and career flexibility. It was also discovered that critical thinking was deemed to be the most important attribute that would help their businesses grow, more than creativity, or improved IT.

Job environments are rapidly shifting into new job positions pressuring workers. Employees will no longer be able to rely on others to make key decisions and will be forced to make them easily and alone.

Good decisions include concentrating on the most relevant information, asking the right questions, and making the right conclusions that too few workers have these skills. In a study of Human Resource Managers (SHRM), it was discovered that a full 70 percent of high school workers lost critical thinking skills. In other recent studies, during the first two years of college, forty-five percent of college graduates made no noticeable improvement in the development of critical thinking or reasoning skills. Thirty-six percent did not show any major gains in critical thinking skills after four years. When these students leave college and enter the workforce, they will not be prepared to meet the working world's challenges. If managers say critical thinking skills are highly valued, candidates exhibiting these skills will be in demand and rare to find. The skills of critical thinking will become invaluable. Certain types of jobs and work environments change, flexibility and adaptability will become crucial to meeting real-world conditions and something that will need to be screened for in interviews by human resources professionals and recruiters. It will also become important to develop the critical thinking skill sets of your existing employees.

One approach for professionals with human resources is to use preliminary hiring thinking assessments. Individuals who score well on these tests display good analytical skills, judgment, decision-making, and performance overall. They often demonstrate the ability to assess the value of the given data, are innovative, have better job skills, and often move up in your company. There are some evaluations for managerial or professional candidates evaluating hard skills. Research also demonstrates that higher-level management positions require critical thinking skills and the ability to quickly learn and accurately process information. Organizations that include both critical thinking and personality testing in hiring practices will have a greater overall candidate perspective than organizations that use personality or critical thinking evaluations alone. Through incorporating probing strategies, it is possible to help workers become tactical thinkers and higher-order thinkers. Better interviewing allows the learner to more efficiently interpret and synthesize data. The method can become automated by repetition with the ultimate goal of transferring information in new situations and scenarios. Some classes teach students not great thinkers or questioners to be good listeners. Passive thinking does not automatically improve cognitive skills or behavioral changes. It will be more successful in participating actively in the learning process and will deliver more long-term outcomes.

Knowledge gained and interpreted by thinking of the higher-order is stored longer than conventional memorization. Knowledge is easier to transfer and implement, resulting in a better solution to problems. Then the questioning becomes a vital part of the process of teaching and learning. Perfecting the questioning art begins with determining what is known and allows the instructor or mentor to develop new ideas and understandings. It is possible to use probing methods to promote students ' ability to think. Create relevant questions. Focus on the technique you use. Encourage interactive discussion and promote engagement. Open-ended questions usually lead the student to more effectively analyze and evaluate. A skilled questioner's most important elements are to ask short and concise questions, rephrasing, and drawing additional answers from the answers of the student.

There is also a need for training to learn every skill. Offer your group the opportunity to practice the ideas, talents, behaviors, and behavioral changes that come from your questions, and choose appropriate experiences that enable them to learn.

Find a scenario that draws on what they already learn when dreaming about circumstances to add a new employee or mentee. It can be as easy as reading a rule, giving an example of a situation in real life, pointing something out on a table or in person. Then model an issue that shows the correct process of thinking. Propose a dilemma that can be overcome by working together or talking through the situation. Also, for exploratory questions, use your inquiry strategy. What would do if that happened? Explain what happened to me? What strategies have worked or have not worked at all? What are you going to do next time? What are we going to do? Perhaps there's a discussion. What's going to happen next? Finally, provide some form of input and create a chance of self-assessment. Use this feedback to build on your next lesson and never forget creative thinking to be rewarded. If they don't feel it is valued, the learners won't want to repeat their behavior.

You will know that when the problem is visualized and can be described and explained, there is higher-order thinking. The learner will also be able to differentiate between relevant and non-relevant information and will search for reasons why something is happening or the root cause. They will rationalize or explain why a solution is going to work and see different angles or sides of a problem. Try to draw on challenges in the real world. This not only lets the student use the data in the correct reference frame, but it also allows you to solve problems in your company or business in the real world. Encourage your learner to think about the strategies you are introducing, as this will reinforce that this is a valuable process to implement when solving problems over and over again. If recruiters and managers begin to look for employees with these skills and use the art of questioning for existing employees, critical thinking will become invaluable to the future success of your organization. There is a competitive advantage for businesses that can recruit and grow critical thinkers. With these capabilities, too few workers are employed, with few finding chances in the workforce to improve them.

Characteristics of Critical Thinkers

Albert Einstein, Henry Ford, Marie Curie, Sigmund Freud, these are just some of the critical thinkers who influenced our modern life. Critical thinkers think clearly and rationally, making logical connections between theories— they are crucial to the discovery and comprehension of the world in which we live.

Critical thinking is more than just the compilation of facts and knowledge; it is a way to approach anything that currently occupies your mind to draw the best possible conclusion. Independent thinkers are constantly focused on improving their skills and investing in independent self-learning. We are making some of the best leaders as they can reach new self-improvement and self-actualization flights.

Cultivate the following 16 characteristics of critical thinkers if you are hoping to reach your full potential and make your mark on the world.

1. Observation

Observation is one of the earliest critical thinking skills we learn as children— it is our ability to understand and perceive the world around us. The capacity to record information and collect data through the senses requires careful observation. Finally, our observations will lead to insight and a deeper understanding of the world.

2. Curiosity

Curiosity is a key feature of many successful rulers. It is a trait for leaders who are critical thinkers to be genuinely inquisitive and interested in the world and the people around you. A curious person will ask why something is the way it is, instead of treating everything at face value.

As we get older, putting aside what might seem like adolescent curiosity is harder. Curiosity encourages you to be open-minded and motivates you to acquire deeper knowledge— all of which is often important to be a lifelong learner.

3. Objectivity

When looking at knowledge or a scenario, good critical thinking should be as objective as possible. We focus on facts and the empirical analysis of the available information.

Objective minds seek to avoid influencing their decision through their feelings (and those of others).

Nevertheless, it is impossible for people to remain entirely impartial because we are all influenced by our opinions, life experiences, and perceptions. Being aware of our prejudices is the first step towards being impartial and looking dispassionately at a question. Once you can get rid of the situation, you can analyze it more thoroughly.

4. Introspection

This is the art of being aware of your thinking— or thinking about how you think about things, to put it another way. Critical thinkers need introspection to be aware of their degree of alertness, attentiveness, and bias. This is your ability to explore your innermost thoughts, beliefs, and perceptions. Introspection is closely related to self-reflection, allowing you insight into your state of mind and feeling.

5. Analytical thinking

Critical thinkers and vice versa are also the best analytical thinkers. If looking at almost anything, whether it is a contract, document, business model, or even a relationship, the ability to analyze data is important.

Information analysis means breaking down information to its parts and evaluating how well those parts work together and separately. The analysis is based on observation, collecting, and analyzing facts so that a valid inference can be drawn. Through objectivity, analytical thinking begins.

6. Identifying biases

Critical thinkers are challenging themselves to identify the evidence that forms their beliefs and to assess whether they are credible or not. Doing so helps you understand your prejudices and challenge your preconceived notions.

This is an important step in becoming mindful of how stereotypes influence your perception and understanding when it is likely to distort data. Ask yourself who benefits from the information when looking at information. Is there a motive for the origins of this information? Does the source ignore data that do not help its arguments or convictions and leaving it out?

7. Determining relevance

One of the most difficult parts of critical thinking is to figure out what is the most relevant, meaningful, and important information for your consideration. In many cases, knowledge that may seem important will be provided to you, but it may turn out to be just a small point of detail to remember.

Ask whether the topic being discussed is theoretically important to a source of information. Is it really helpful and impartial, or is it just distracted from a more relevant topic?

8. Inference

The information does not always come with a summary that explains exactly what it means. Critical thinkers need to assess information based on raw data and draw conclusions. The inference is the capacity to extrapolate significance of information and, when analyzing a situation, to uncover potential results.

Understanding the difference between inferences and assumptions is also important. For example, if you see information weighing 260 pounds, you might believe that they are overweight and unhealthy. Nevertheless, this assumption may be changed by other data points, such as height and body structure.

9. Compassion and compassion.

To critical thinkers, possessing compassion and empathy may seem a detriment. Sentimental and emotional being may, after all, skew our perception of a situation. But the essence of empathy is to be worried about others and respect other people's welfare.

Without empathy, from dark, heartless statistical facts and data, we can interpret both knowledge and circumstances. Letting our cynicism become toxic and being suspicious of everything we look at would be easy. But we must also take into account the human element to be a good critical thinker. Not all we do is about isolated information and data— it's about individuals as well.

10. Humility

Humility is the ability to accept one's shortcomings and correctly perceive one's positive attributes. You are aware of your shortcomings, but also your strengths when you have humility, and this is an important element in critical thinking and willingness to stretch and open your mind.

You are open to the viewpoints of other people when you have intellectual humility, and you recognize when you are wrong, and you are willing to challenge your own beliefs when necessary.

11. Ready to challenge the status quo.

Critical thinking involves challenging long-established business processes and refusing to follow traditional methods merely because that's how it was always done. Critical thinkers are looking for intelligent, thoughtful answers and methods that take into account all the information and practices currently available and relevant to them. They may seem controversial about their willingness to challenge the status quo, but it is an essential part of a critical thinker's creative and innovative mind.

12. Open-mindedness
This allows critical thinkers to see the broader view of being able to step back from a situation and not become involved. Critical thinkers avoid getting into or taking sides in a frenzied debate— they want to consider both views. Critical thinkers are not jumping to conclusions. With an open mind, we address a problem or circumstance and accept certain views and opinions.

13. That's wrong. Conscious of common mistakes in planning.
Critical thinkers do not allow illusions and misunderstandings to cloud their logic and reasoning.

We are aware of common logical errors, which are errors in thought, frequently sneaking into statements and discussions. Some common mistakes in thinking include:

- ➢ Circular reasoning, which uses the premise of an argument or a conclusion to support the argument itself.
- ➢ Intellectual workaround bias, where you stubbornly adhere to a favorite perspective or statement when there are other, more powerful options or theories.
- ➢ Confusing causal correlation. In other terms, saying that one triggers the other when two things happen together. This assumption is not justified without direct evidence.

14. Creative thinking

There are also largely creative thinkers who are effective critical thinkers. For problem-solving, creative thinkers ignore conventional frameworks— they think outside the box. We have a wide variety of interests and work on an issue from multiple perspectives. We are also open to experimenting with different approaches and different points of view.

The greatest difference between critical thinkers and creative thinkers is that imagination is synonymous with the creation of ideas, while critical thinking is correlated with the study and assessment of these ideas. To bring in new ideas, imagination is important; critical thinking will bring these ideas into sharper focus.

15. Good communicators

In many situations, interpersonal problems are focused on an inability to critically think or see a problem from different perspectives. Effective communication starts with a simple method of thought.

Critical thinking is the device we use to create and articulate our ideas in a coherent manner. Critical thinking is based on following the thinking process or line of reasoning of another person. A successful critical thinker must be able to impressively express his or her thoughts and then interpret others ' responses.

16. Active listeners

Critical thinkers don't just want to communicate their point to others; they are also careful to engage in active listening and listen to the points of view of others.

They are actively trying to participate rather than being a passive listener during a conversation or discussion.
To help them differentiate evidence from theories, they ask questions. They collect information and gain feedback by answering open-ended questions which explore the problem more closely.

How To Think Logically

Have you ever wished to have the ability to solve problems both successfully and easily? If so, be much more rational, you might want to improve your thinking patterns.

Did you see Sherlock's new TV show, played this time by the brilliant Benedict Cumberbatch? If you have, you're probably envy his impressive deduction abilities and thinking, "Why is he doing this?". The truth is you can do it as well.

Okay, maybe you can't solve a complex murder case, but with the objective of promoting problem-solving and decision making, you could improve your logical thinking. In return, these skills will usually lead to your career and life success.

Here are some tricks and techniques that can motivate you to make your mind clearer.

Making Logical Conclusions

Although it may sound stupid to you, try to think in conditional statements and find small and perhaps insignificant facts causes and consequences. For starters, let's say it's cold outside every time it's snowing. The expression would say: "If it snows, outside it's freezing."

If the assumption (the first part of the sentence) is true in conditional sentences, then the inference (the second part) is also true. Attempt to do that with other things also (if I drop my mobile, it's going to get ruined; if I don't eat, I'm going to get starving, etc.) and see if that premise partnership or assumption still fits vice versa.

Play Card Games

Who said it must be difficult to sharpen your logical thinking? It's the reverse. Gather your mates once a week and play card games to stimulate your brain to think easily and clearly. Not only are competitive card games good for the soul and enjoyable, but they can also improve memory, concentration, and analytical skills.

They're much better when you add technique into that mixture. Children can play Crazy Eight or Go Fish fun games, while adults can play Black Jack and Poker.

Make Math Fun

There's no question that math is one of the best exercises to improve your analytical skills. Nevertheless, it can be an unattractive pastime for both children and adults.

Fortunately, there are a lot of fun ways to work on your math for you.

Through math games on different websites or using smartphone apps, both grown-ups and children can find enjoyment and mental challenges.

Playing Sudoku and other activities that include dealing with numbers in enjoyable and interesting ways will potentially improve the ability of the mind to solve real issues quickly.

Solve Mysteries and Break Codes

Writing crime stories and novels by police allows readers to think critically. Through watching these movies or TV shows, you can get a similar experience. Try to solve a certain mystery before the story's protagonist.

Don't be disappointed if it doesn't go as you expected it would. Just remember from the beginning of this article the words of the famous hero: "When you eliminate the impossible, whatever remains, however unlikely, must be the truth." So remove the impossible and the unlikely, and the solution will come to you. Another great brain activity is cracking codes (created by your buddies or found on the web).

Conduct a Debate

Have you ever been in dispute when you can't find the right arguments to explain why something is good or bad? We've all done it.

Debates are good as they allow you to look out causes and consequences, turn them into strong arguments, and find the reasoning behind them all.

Because they need to think logically and make on-the-go decisions, discussions can sharpen your mind. So you can either join a chat group or hold a conversation about economics, art, culture, literature, etc. with your family.

Be Strategic

Since logical thinking is all about putting together the pieces, strategic thinking plays an important role in this process. Being a strategic thinker will not only overcharge the mind, but it will also be a useful asset to work-related choices and even to the success of personal life. For this reason, some of the fundamental behaviors you can develop are planning (thinking about what is to come), critical thinking (questioning everything), analyzing (seeking patterns), determining (concluding), and improving (from your mistakes).

Play strategy games (board games, card games, video games, etc.) and design a strategy for sporting events to sharpen your strategic thinking.

Just as it is important to find your internal peace and focus on your faith, it is also important to keep your mind continually busy with challenging games and activities, so you can develop your rational thinking, which is vital for a productive and therefore harmonious existence.

Evaluate your memory

Your brain boosts with workout like any other part of your body. To evaluate your recall is a fantastic method of offering exercise to your brain. See the number of details of a given minute, schedule, or work that you can keep in mind throughout the day.

Try to memorize small things every day. Set up a guide of food and dedicate it to memory as well. Memorize a brief passage from a poem or novel. Wait for an hour and see how much of what you have dedicated to memory you can remember.

Draw a memory map.

A map from your home to work, a restaurant, the home of a close friend, or another place you regularly visit.

Notice the details.
Making a conscious attempt to identify things that are relatively pointless can be a good tool to help you become much more rational. Watch the new journal diminished on the hand of your good friend? Should you list your school and college's actions? Search for mistakes of punctuation in the texts? If the answer is no, it would be a fun time to start at the moment. The more you process, the better your mind is going to be. You're going to end up being a more vital thinker over time.

Other Tricks include:
Based on logical thinking, the reading. Practice in your reading to use inductive or deductive logic — Evite common mistakes.

INDUCTIVE REASONING: You start with several instances (facts or observations) when you reason inductively and use them to draw a general conclusion. You think inductively if you perceive facts. Using the likelihood of generalizing is called an inductive leap. Therefore, inductive claims are intended to produce likely and plausible hypotheses rather than to produce certainty. Your reader draws the inference you hope to draw when your proof mounts.

You should ensure that the amount of evidence is adequate and not dependent on analysis that is extraordinary or skewed. Make sure you haven't omitted facts that invalidate the argument (called the "neglected aspect") and given just evidence supporting a predetermined conclusion (called "slanting").

DEDUCTIVE REASONING: You begin with generalizations (premises) if you think deductively and extend them to a particular instance to conclude that instance. Deductive reasoning also involves syllogism, a line of thought consisting of a major premise, a minor premise, and a conclusion; for example, all people are foolish (major premise); Smith is a man (minor premise); thus, Smith is foolish (conclusion). For example, to accept the argument, the reader should accept the concepts and principles that you choose as assumptions. There is no discussion of assumptions occasionally. It is important to analyze a syllogism with an unstated major or minor assumption, or even an unstated inference, because the excluded assertion may constitute an incorrect generalization.

THE TOULMIN Approach: The Toulmin approach is another way to view the mechanism of logical thinking. This model is less restricted than the syllogism and allows for the important elements of probability, support, or proof of the reader's objections ' premise and rebuttal. This approach sees claims as going from agreed facts or evidence (data) to an inference (claim) through an assertion (warrant) forming a fair relationship between the two. The warrant is often implied in arguments, and to be acceptable, as is the unstated premise in the syllogism. The author may cause a big assumption to be expected. Qualifiers like probably, possibly, doubtless, and surely show the degree of certainty of the conclusion; refutational terms like unless the writer allows objections to be anticipated.

FALLACIES: There must be both a plausible and real deductive stated. A real argument is based on well-backed assumptions that are generally accepted. Learn to distinguish between fact and opinion (based on personal preferences) (based on verifiable data). A valid argument fits a pattern of reasonable thought.

Fallacies are flaws in (truth) and logic (validity) assumptions. They may result from misuse or misrepresentation of evidence, relying on defective premises or omitting a necessary premise, or distorting the issues. Some of the major forms of fallacies are as follows:

Non-Sequitur: a statement that does not logically follow from what has just been said; in other words, a conclusion that does not follow from the premises.
Hasty generalization: a generalization based on insufficient evidence or exceptional or biased evidence.

Ad Hominem: Question the individual posing a question rather than dealing with the problem itself objectively.

Bandwagon: An argument that says, "Everyone does and does and believes that, so you should." Red Herring: Dodging the real issue by drawing attention to an irrelevant issue. Claiming that there are only two options when there are more than two. False Analogy: The belief that in some cases, if two events are the same, they have to be unique.

Equivocation: an inference that in two different senses is wrongly dependent on the use of a word.

Slippery Slope: The belief that it will be the first step in a downward spiral if one element is approved.

Oversimplification: A comment or point that leaves relevant issues out.

Pleading for Question: a statement reaffirming the point that has just been made. Such a statement is conditional in that a point mentioned in the assumption is taken as an inference.

Benefits Of Critical Thinking And Why They Matter

How often do you hear the question, "Come down to earth and think critically?" It is likely common to hear from family, students, teachers, and other people who have already seen the world and can agree that the practice of consciously learning about a subject or concept without having feelings or opinions to influence you is the best way to deal with this environment. But is it valid at all times? The essay attempts to provide you with both the benefits of critical thinking and its drawbacks with a rational answer to these questions. Make confident that in everyday life you can discover the golden mean of using critical thinking skills.

One Side of the Coin: 5 Advantages of Critical Thinking

➢ The ability to think logically and rationally;

> The ability to interpret facts objectively;
> The ability to understand the logical connection between ideas;
> The ability to make informed decisions, etc.

Let's find out why it is considered useful for these abilities.

1. You Are Able to Evaluate Issues without Bias

Most people approach things differently–one depends on their values, perceptions, feelings, or the thoughts of somebody else. All this influences how you deal with one issue or another, especially with such controversial topics as abortion, death penalty, animal testing, or immigration. With solid evidence, there are many questions to be answered. And what's going to help you get it? Yes, critical thinking lets you collect and analyze relevant information and accurately translate it for sound conclusions and solutions.

2. You Can Foresee How Things Will Turn out

Willpower, intelligence, expertise, inspiration, understanding of the right people, being in the right place, and time is all that makes a person successful in the modern world.

And yet, there's another aspect that allows progress to be accomplished—it's the ability to predict what's going to happen and need in the future. How can it be? Analytically and critically, you know the current issues by recognizing the logical connections between ideas and arguments. For example, Heather A. Butler researched 244 participants with her collaborators, Christopher Pentoney, Mabelle P. Bong, to investigate the importance of critical thinking and intellectual to forecasting real-world outcomes. As a consequence, it is known that critical thinking is a better predictor of real-world outcomes than knowledge. So start developing your critical thinking skills right now to know what's going to happen in various important areas—economics, industry, advertising, sales, etc.

3. You Communicate with Others Sharing Your Ideas Effectively

It is crucial to get a message out to the target audience–be it your boss, peers, or professors–when you analyze a question and forecast the possible outcomes. Critical thinking usually detaches all our thoughts from the public expression of an argument.

Only have a realistic view of the situation at hand and how to solve a problem by collaborating with friends or other individuals together. Simultaneously, open mind for a different view that you can also perceive with the help of recognizing valid logic.

4. You Are Trusted to Figure Out Solutions to Complex Problems

It is particularly valuable when a person can define, evaluate problems and even systematically predict and solve them rather than by intuition or instinct. You still have to hope for the best–for example, once you have faith in executing complex tasks in a business. In this case, it means that you are guaranteed career promotion. It will also have an overall impact on your life. Indeed, addressing complex issues is a great responsibility. But imagine how many difficult questions you might be able to answer if you put your critical thinking skills into practice.

5. You are highly appreciated by employers

If critical thinking is one of your attributes, you have already been demonstrated the opportunities in a professional career.

What do students usually do when they graduate from college or university? "Where can I find my dream job?" For students, this is a common question. That's why in critical thinking if you want to excel immediately in a job search, continue to succeed. If an HR expert sees your strong critical thinking skills in resumes, cover letters, or during job interviews, make sure that most of the doors to top business firms are open to you. Many firms search for critical thinkers, communicative, constructive, and innovative career candidates.

The Flip Side to the Coin: 5 Disadvantages of Critical Thinking

Critical thinking is considered as important as breathing in some situations. Like in an interview, or perhaps when you do a test, but not always. In childhood, when you were asked, "What would you like to be?" and you might automatically answer,' I want to be a journalist when I grow up,' or' I dream of becoming an artist,' but then you grew up, and all the innocence and positive outlook were destroyed when life's realities and practicalities crashed against you.

Critical thinking is the dream-killer. One minute you'll dream of being the greatest artist of all times, and you'll notice the huge, gaping holes in your plan when you start to analyze it critically. You're going to start having second thoughts and facing endless dilemmas. Are you going to have to move to another city? Have you the ability to become an artist? Are you competitive? The list continues and continues.

You may be proud of your ability to think critically at any stage, but here are some examples that can be detrimental to you.

1. Your Peers' Jokes Are Not Funny Anymore

It can be a surreal experience to hang out with your friends. But when you analyze everything, all of a sudden, their jokes make no sense to you, and they are no longer funny. How many times have you rolled your eyes at them because you automatically think "amateur hour" when you hear one of their repeated jokes!" and you're just frowning when they want you to smile.

2. You care too much about gender equality

If your girlfriend/boyfriend gushes over that amazing invitation you received to a party to come, and you forget about gender equality. Don't you think you have a little different idea?

3. You Feel Shame When Your Group Mates Speak

And when, as you would have thought, they are unable to express their thoughts in a reasonable, so intelligent manner, you feel sorry for your group mates and simultaneously feel ashamed that you talk about them this way and that you are like that.

4. You're alone with your books

Not only do you love novels, your mates will hate, but you can't talk to them about the finer points in the story because they'll probably think you've gone crazy. And they're smiling at you.

5. You Only Adequate Companion Is You

It's hard to admit, but you can only talk to yourself about really interesting issues. Who can think about climate change's biocultural approach?

Who knows why promoting solar energy is important? Who is defending Severus Snape for doing everything he can to protect Harry? Sure, you alone.

Okay, all in all, critical thinking has its benefits and is quite useful in some situations (think about Sherlock Holmes, guys!). But most of the time, it will leach out all the fun and exasperate the mates around you.

Businesses that want to remain competitive and profitable need to recruit critically thinking workers. Hiring a college graduate is not enough. New hires must be knowledgeable, logical, and strong problem-solvers. Strategic and critical thinking is the most needed skill by employers worldwide when evaluating job candidates, according to business surveys. The U.S. Labor Department has listed critical thinking, problem-solving, decision-making, organizational strategy, and risk management as essential workplace skills. Employers demand that recruits have more than textbook knowledge and technical skills, and agree that critical thinking is vital for job performance and career mobility. It was also revealed that critical thinking was considered the most important attribute to help their businesses grow, more than creativity or increased information technology.

Job conditions are increasingly pushing workers into new jobs. Employees can no longer rely on others to make key decisions and are forced to make them alone and quickly. Good decisions include concentrating on the most relevant information, asking the right questions, and believing correctly that too few workers possess these skills. A survey of Human Resource professionals (SHRM) found a total 70 percent of high school workers are deficient in critical thinking skills. In other recent studies, 45 percent of college graduates made no noticeable improvement in developing critical thinking or reasoning skills during college's first two years. After four years, 36% made no major gains in critical thinking skills. When these students leave school and enter the workforce, they will be unprepared for working world challenges. When managers say critical thinking skills are highly valued, applicants possessing these qualities will be in demand and difficult to find. Critical skills will become invaluable. The types of jobs and work environments evolve, versatility and adaptability will become essential to meeting real-world conditions and something that practitioners and recruiters need to test for in interviews. Developing critical thinking sets of your existing employees will also become important.

One strategy for management managers is to use pre-hiring planning tests. Individuals who score well on these assessments demonstrate good analytical skills, reasoning, decision-making, and efficiency. They often demonstrate the ability to evaluate the information value presented, are innovative, have better job knowledge, and often move up in your business. There are some tests of managerial and skilled applicants assessing hard skills. Research also shows that higher-level management roles require critical thinking skills and the ability to learn quickly and accurately process information. Organizations that include both critical thinking and personality tests in hiring practices will have a greater overall candidate perspective than organizations that use personality or critical thinking assessments alone. Helping employees become strategic thinkers can be done by introducing questioning techniques. Better questioning helps to visualize better and synthesize information. By practice, this process can become automatic, with the ultimate goal of transferring information to new situations and scenarios. Some courses teach students to be good listeners, not great thinkers.

Passive training does not inherently improve mental or behavioral skills. Active participation in the learning process will be more successful, providing more long-term results. Knowledge acquired and interpreted by higher-order thought is recalled more than conventional memorization. Knowledge is easier to transfer and implement, leading to better problem-solving. Questioning becomes a vital part of teaching and learning. Perfecting the questioning art begins with establishing what is known, allowing the instructor or mentor to develop new ideas and understandings. Questioning strategies can be used to promote students ' mentality. Create appropriate questions. Perform the strategy. Encourage open dialogue and participation. Generally, open-ended questions lead students to explore and assess more effectively. A professional questioner's most important elements are asking short and concise questions, rephrasing, and extracting more responses from the student's answers. The practice must also master every ability. Offer your audience the opportunity to practice the ideas, skills, behaviors, and behavioral changes resulting from your questions and choose specific activities to enable them to reflect.

Think of scenarios to bring your new employee or mentee to a scenario that builds on what they already know.

It can be as easy as reading a rule, providing a real-life example of a situation, pointing something on a table or in person. Instead design a problem showing the right thought process. Propose a problem that can be solved collaboratively or through the scenario. Also, use an exploratory interrogation method. What if it were? Explain what just happened? What strategies worked or didn't work? What'd you do next time? What can we suppose? Maybe there's a discussion. What will happen next? Ultimately, provide some feedback or create opportunities for self-assessment. Use this advice to draw on your next lesson and never lose creative thinking. Learners won't want to replicate their actions unless they feel valued. You'll know that when the problem is visualized, higher-order thought can be represented and clarified. The learner will also be able to distinguish between relevant and non-relevant data and will look for reasons why or why something is happening. You will rationalize and clarify why a solution works and see different angles or sides of a problem.

Recall capitalizing on real-world situations. This not only helps students use the data in the right reference frame but also helps you solve real-world problems in your company or business. Encourage your learner to think about the methods you're implementing, as this will demonstrate that this is a valuable method to adopt while solving problems over and over. If recruiters and managers start looking for employees with these skills and use the art of questioning for existing employees, critical thinking becomes invaluable for the future success of your organization. Companies hiring and developing critical thinkers have a competitive advantage. With these skills being hired, too few employees have opportunities to develop them in the workplace.

Evaluating Patterns of Thinking
Wisdom is adapting knowledge and experience to a given situation to make sound decisions. It's how we relate our awareness (how we know) and experience (what we've been through) to what we do (acting), what we feel (perception) and how we measure (judging).

Wisdom means adding what we've heard. It's studying part-time. Therefore, wisdom comes from (an application). Without doing what we've heard, we can't get understanding. You can't read wisdom; you can't memorize wisdom; you can't repeat wisdom; you can't learn wisdom; you can only gain wisdom by practicing what you've written, memorized, studied and recited. Only by doing can one gain knowledge. Knowledge cannot be gained by silence (idleness); knowledge must be used (applied) before it can be attained.

Wisdom is part of a sequence of events associated with increasing our mental capacity and memory. It is located in the second stage of our human intellectual development; it is amid two other interrelated elements in which one's psychological and intellectual ability cannot be fully explored or utilized. To learn how to receive knowledge, you must first consider how it applies and relies on two other factors complementing it.

That refers to the three foundations of intellectual development.

LEARNING: this is the first step towards cognitive and mental development. This is how increasing cognitive or intellectual growth begins; it is described as a deliberate attempt to acquire specific information on a topic or problem. Put data acquisition. Education is collecting, gaining, or learning knowledge or information. Therefore, each learning process results in the collection or acquiring of knowledge or information. All you'll ever get from learning is intelligence, which means information. That is, data is preserved and processed upon finishing the learning process. Therefore, the outcome of any education you go through is to gain knowledge on some topic or problem. Knowledge ownership doesn't necessarily mean you're wise or clever, and it just means you're knowledgeable, and intelligence carrier. As the old saying goes, he who understands and doesn't understand what he does is no different than he who doesn't know or can't. This is why learning (knowledge) alone is not enough to achieve a high level of intellectual and mental ability. The need for action that gets us to the second stage of our path towards cognitive and mental development; the stage of doing or applying (wisdom).

DOING: this is where the first step of your path towards cognitive and mental development will be triggered. Because learning seeks to gain knowledge or information, the learned knowledge is typically in a dormant state waiting to be triggered. All you have experienced, either through reading, interpretation or experience, is equal to nothing unless it is done or used (applied). The importance of learning is not in gaining facts or expertise, but in its functional utility when applicable in real-time situations and circumstances. This is the source of wisdom, intelligence, and understanding added. To gain wisdom, one must first acquire knowledge or information by reading, only then can one enable what has been learned to receive the wisdom therein.

Wisdom consists in right-applied knowledge or information. Learning something by reading (knowledge) is quite different from knowing something by doing something (wisdom). All acts ' result is different. While it's true you can't have one without the other, and it's equally true that both yield two significantly different results. The do phase is very important to one's psychological and intellectual development because it is the ability to internalize and personalize what has been taught.

The doing stage allows you to bring life into what was dormant, making you a creator rather than an information or knowledge holder.

As we incorporate what we read, we are smarter as we obtain deeper insight from using the inactive iteration of knowledge or information gained into something more concrete and effective.

This is where knowledge or information is transformed from a dormant (passive) resource into a practical (active) resource. When we learn our goal shouldn't be to know, our goal must also be to use (apply) what we've known. That's how to receive knowledge. Why is knowledge so important to developmentally and intellectually? I cannot attain understanding without wisdom. Thus, in our journey towards mental or intellectual development, we reach the final process; understanding.

UNDERSTANDING: the interpretation of knowledge and experience to gain or grasp its meaning. Knowing is your understanding of the awareness, insight, and facts gained in a practical situation or scenario.

It is-rayed through your mindset. To understand better, reading (knowledge) and doing (wisdom) more will broaden your mindset. Understanding comes only when you've done what you've read. In other words, understanding comes only when you have to make use of what you've learned before. That is, only a wise person can achieve knowledge because knowing comes after you have learned.

KNOWLEDGE (learning); WISDOM (doing); UNDERSTANDING (interpretation).

Training encourages us to know what to do, experience equips us to do, while learning helps us to perceive and puts into perspective what we have learned and achieved. Knowing is where we view and bring knowledge (what we learned) and understanding (what we did).

Conclusion

When understood and practiced effectively, critical thinking is a powerful tool. It is important to understand more about the event and mechanism that involves it when developing critical thinking skills. Once acknowledged, concerns about the successful application of critical thinking abilities are likely to dissipate. Critical thinking can turn the process of reasoning into a straightforward, convincing, honest language, carefully and logically designed. At the same time, experiences and responses can be transformed into theories, thoughts, observations, conclusions, inferences, hypotheses, questions, opinions, premises and logical arguments.

There are many misunderstandings about critical thinking that continue to discourage people from actively learning to improve it. Unfortunately, many assume that the process is too difficult and remain unenlightened as to how the process can help them in their personal lives as well as in their work environments.

If you have gone through the proper process of understanding the problem, looking at all possible options, gathering information for the solutions, and evaluating everything, you should rest assured that you should be able to stand alone in the decision you are going to make. You're putting your critical thinking skills into practice by going through this whole process. As with other things that are done for the very first time, it may seem unorthodox, but as you continue to practice these techniques, your critical thinking skills will grow and evolve more.

You need to understand that, generally speaking, the ability to think critically varies from person to person based on their level of exposure to the different issues and how well they managed to solve them. The good thing is that you can learn and develop the ability to think critically and make the most of it.

www.ingramcontent.com/pod-product-compliance
Lightning Source LLC
Chambersburg PA
CBHW070834250726
48662CB00003B/1215